How to Pay Off Your Mortgage Fast Without Sacrificing Your Lifestyle

Proven Mortgage Payoff Strategies That Accelerate Equity While Keeping Cash Flow Strong

By Joseph G. Correa

Copyright & Legal Notice

Published by Live Stronger Faster

First Edition, 2026

Table of Contents

Introduction

For millions of people, the mortgage payment is the single largest monthly expense they will ever have. It often follows them for decades, quietly shaping their lifestyle, financial decisions, stress levels, retirement timeline, and even their ability to pursue opportunities. Many homeowners assume that carrying a mortgage for thirty years is simply part of life. They believe the only options are to either make the minimum payment every month or somehow come up with an enormous amount of money to pay the loan off early. What most people never realize is that there are strategic, intelligent, and realistic ways to dramatically reduce the life of a mortgage without destroying cash flow, sacrificing enjoyment, or living under constant financial pressure.

This book was created to challenge the traditional thinking surrounding mortgages and long-term debt. Too often, homeowners are taught to accept decades of interest payments as unavoidable. They are rarely shown how small adjustments, strategic planning, and disciplined financial habits can save hundreds of thousands of dollars and potentially eliminate years—or even decades—off their mortgage timeline. Even worse, many people become so focused on surviving their monthly bills that they never step back to analyze how their mortgage fits into their overall wealth-building strategy.

The goal of this book is not simply to help you pay off a house faster. The goal is to help you create freedom. Financial freedom is not only about having money in the bank. It is about reducing obligations, lowering stress, increasing flexibility, and gaining control over your future. A mortgage can either become a lifelong burden that limits your options or a carefully managed financial tool that accelerates wealth creation and long-term stability. The difference often comes down to knowledge, strategy, and execution.

One of the biggest myths in personal finance is that paying off a mortgage early automatically requires extreme sacrifice. Many people imagine living a miserable lifestyle, eliminating all enjoyment, refusing vacations, never dining out, and obsessively cutting every expense just to make extra mortgage payments. While discipline is certainly important, aggressive financial suffering is not the only path to mortgage freedom. In reality, sustainable strategies often work far better than extreme short-term sacrifices that lead to burnout, frustration, or financial instability.

This book focuses specifically on how to pay off your mortgage fast while keeping your lifestyle intact. That means learning how to optimize cash flow, use strategic payments intelligently, leverage financial opportunities, and make smarter long-term decisions without feeling financially trapped. The strategies inside this book are designed for real people with real lives, families, responsibilities, goals, and unexpected expenses. You do not need to become financially obsessed to make meaningful progress. You simply need a system that works consistently over time.

One of the most powerful concepts you will learn throughout this series is that mortgages are heavily front-loaded with interest. In the early years of a traditional mortgage, a significant portion of each monthly payment goes toward interest rather than principal reduction. Many homeowners are shocked when they discover how slowly their balance declines during the first decade of ownership. Understanding how amortization works is one of the first major steps toward taking control of your financial future.

When you understand the mechanics behind mortgage interest, you begin to see opportunities that most homeowners completely miss. Small additional principal payments, strategic refinancing decisions, improved cash flow management, biweekly payment systems, and targeted lump-sum reductions can dramatically accelerate mortgage payoff timelines. In some cases, homeowners can save tens or even hundreds of thousands of dollars in interest simply by making minor strategic adjustments that barely impact their lifestyle.

However, this book is not about blindly paying off debt at all costs. There are times when accelerating mortgage payoff makes tremendous financial sense, and there are times when maintaining liquidity and investing elsewhere may create greater overall wealth. Financial success is not about emotional decision-making. It is about understanding trade-offs, opportunities, risk management, and long-term goals. This series was designed to help you think strategically rather than emotionally about your mortgage.

Throughout this book, you will learn how to balance mortgage acceleration with cash flow preservation. Cash flow is the lifeblood of financial flexibility. A homeowner who aggressively throws every dollar toward their mortgage while neglecting emergency savings, retirement investing, or liquidity may actually increase financial vulnerability rather than reduce it. True financial intelligence requires balance. You want to reduce debt while simultaneously strengthening your overall financial foundation.

This book was also written for people at different stages of life and income levels. Whether you recently purchased your first home, are halfway through a thirty-year mortgage, own multiple properties, or are simply looking for ways to optimize your financial future, the principles inside this book can be adapted to your situation. Some readers may focus on eliminating debt as quickly as possible for peace of mind. Others may prioritize flexibility while still accelerating equity growth. There is no single perfect strategy for everyone, which is why understanding multiple approaches is so important.

In today's economy, financial uncertainty has become increasingly common. Interest rates fluctuate, inflation impacts purchasing power, job markets change, and unexpected expenses can appear at any time. Many homeowners feel trapped between wanting to eliminate debt and needing to maintain financial security. This is precisely why intelligent mortgage management matters more than ever before. A strong strategy can create resilience, stability, and long-term opportunity even during uncertain economic periods.

Another important principle discussed throughout this series is the emotional impact of debt. While mortgages are often considered "good debt," they still create ongoing obligations and financial pressure. Many homeowners underestimate the psychological relief that comes from reducing long-term liabilities. Lower debt obligations can improve sleep, reduce anxiety, increase confidence, and provide greater freedom to pursue personal and professional goals. Financial health is not just mathematical—it is emotional and behavioral as well.

At the same time, this series recognizes that wealth-building is multifaceted. Simply becoming debt-free does not automatically create wealth. A person with no mortgage but no investments, savings, or income-producing assets may still struggle financially. This is why the Mortgage Payoff & Wealth Acceleration Series goes beyond basic debt reduction. It explores how mortgage strategies interact with investing, cash flow, real estate acquisition, tax planning, and long-term financial independence.

As you move through this book, you will notice that the focus is on practical implementation rather than theoretical concepts alone. Financial knowledge without action rarely changes outcomes. The strategies discussed are intended to be understandable, actionable, and adaptable. You will learn not only why certain strategies work, but how to apply them based on your own goals, income, expenses, and risk tolerance.

One of the major themes you will encounter repeatedly is intentionality. Many people drift through decades of mortgage payments without a plan. They simply pay whatever the lender tells them to pay and hope things eventually work out. Wealthy and financially disciplined individuals tend to approach mortgages differently. They actively manage debt, analyze opportunities, monitor cash flow, and make strategic adjustments over time. The difference between financial stagnation and financial acceleration often comes down to intentional decision-making.

You will also learn that time is one of the most powerful financial assets you possess. Even relatively small changes made consistently over long periods can create enormous results. An extra payment here, a refinance at the right moment there, strategic budgeting adjustments, or intelligent use of additional income can compound into life-changing savings over time. Mortgage acceleration is often less about dramatic one-time actions and more about consistent strategic behavior.

This series is designed to progressively expand your understanding of mortgage optimization and wealth acceleration. In this first book, the focus is on establishing the foundation—how to pay off your mortgage faster without sacrificing your quality of life. Future books will explore more advanced concepts such as biweekly payment systems, refinancing strategies, leveraging cash flow, using rental income, high-income optimization methods, and balancing mortgage payoff with real estate investing and long-term wealth creation.

The reality is that financial freedom rarely happens by accident. It is usually the result of intentional education, consistent execution, disciplined habits, and long-term thinking. Mortgages can either delay financial independence or become part of a larger strategy that accelerates it. The outcome depends largely on how you manage the debt, structure your finances, and align your actions with your goals.

By reading this book, you are already taking an important step toward greater financial awareness and control. You are choosing to learn strategies that many homeowners never discover until it is too late. More importantly, you are beginning to shift from passive financial behavior to active financial leadership over your own life.

The journey toward mortgage freedom does not require perfection. It requires progress. Small strategic improvements made consistently over time can produce extraordinary long-term results. Whether your goal is to eliminate your mortgage early, reduce financial stress, increase cash flow, retire sooner, build wealth, or simply gain more options in life, the principles inside this book are designed to help you move closer to that reality.

Your mortgage does not have to control your future. With the right strategy, discipline, and mindset, it can become one of the most powerful stepping stones toward long-term financial freedom and wealth acceleration.

Chapter 1

Understanding the True Cost of a Mortgage and Why Most People Stay in Debt Too Long

For many homeowners, a mortgage feels normal. It becomes part of life in the same way utilities, insurance, groceries, and taxes become recurring obligations. People buy homes with the expectation that they will make payments for thirty years, and over time they stop questioning whether there may be a faster, smarter, or more financially strategic way to handle the debt. The mortgage payment becomes automatic, and many homeowners spend decades simply accepting the process without fully understanding how much the loan truly costs them over time.

One of the biggest financial mistakes people make is focusing only on the monthly payment instead of the total cost of borrowing. Mortgage lenders often structure loans in a way that makes the payment appear manageable and attractive, but very few borrowers stop to calculate the total amount of interest they will eventually pay over the life of the loan. A mortgage may seem affordable month-to-month, yet the long-term financial impact can be enormous. For example, a homeowner who borrows $400,000 at a fixed interest rate over thirty years may ultimately repay hundreds of thousands of dollars in interest alone. In many cases, borrowers end up paying nearly double the original amount borrowed by the time the mortgage is fully repaid. This is one of the primary reasons why understanding mortgage structure is critical for long-term financial success. When homeowners realize how interest accumulates over time, they begin to understand why strategic mortgage payoff planning matters so much.

One of the most important concepts in mortgage financing is amortization. Amortization refers to the way mortgage payments are structured over time. In the early years of a mortgage, the majority of the payment goes toward interest rather than reducing the principal balance. This surprises many homeowners because they assume each payment significantly reduces what they owe. In reality, early mortgage payments often make only a small dent in the principal balance while heavily benefiting the lender through interest collection.

This is why many homeowners feel frustrated after making payments for years only to discover they still owe nearly the same amount they originally borrowed. Without understanding amortization, people may unknowingly remain trapped in debt far longer than necessary. However, once borrowers understand how the system works, they can begin using strategies that attack principal more aggressively and reduce total interest costs substantially.

The problem is not necessarily the mortgage itself. A mortgage can be an extremely valuable financial tool when used correctly. Homeownership can provide stability, appreciation potential, tax advantages, and long-term equity growth. The real issue is that most borrowers never develop a strategic plan for managing the mortgage efficiently. They simply follow the default thirty-year schedule without considering alternatives.

Lenders are not primarily focused on helping borrowers eliminate debt quickly. Their business model depends heavily on long-term interest payments. This does not make lenders unethical, but it does mean homeowners must take personal responsibility for understanding how loans operate and how to manage them strategically. Financial education becomes one of the most powerful tools a homeowner can possess.

Another reason people stay in mortgage debt too long is lifestyle inflation. As income rises, many individuals increase spending just as quickly. Larger homes, newer vehicles, luxury purchases, dining out, vacations, subscriptions, and consumer debt often absorb any additional income that could otherwise be used to build wealth or reduce liabilities. Instead of accelerating mortgage payoff, many people unintentionally create lifestyles that require continued high monthly obligations.

Modern society often encourages consumption rather than financial efficiency. People are constantly exposed to marketing designed to make them spend more, borrow more, and upgrade more frequently. Financial discipline becomes difficult when external pressure continuously pushes consumers toward larger lifestyles. This is one reason why so many high-income earners still struggle financially despite earning substantial incomes. Income alone does not create wealth. Financial management does.

The reality is that a homeowner earning $80,000 annually with disciplined financial habits may build more long-term wealth than someone earning $250,000 annually who constantly increases expenses and debt obligations. Mortgage acceleration is not always about earning dramatically more money. Often, it is about improving financial awareness, reducing waste, and directing cash flow intentionally.

Fear also keeps many people trapped in long-term debt cycles. Some homeowners believe making extra mortgage payments will leave them financially vulnerable. Others assume they need massive amounts of money before paying down debt aggressively. While maintaining liquidity and emergency savings is extremely important, many borrowers underestimate the power of small consistent actions. Even modest additional principal payments can create significant long-term savings when applied consistently over time.

For example, adding a relatively small amount toward principal each month may remove several years from a mortgage term while saving tens of thousands of dollars in interest. This happens because extra principal payments reduce the loan balance directly, which decreases the amount of future interest charged. The earlier these reductions occur, the greater the long-term impact becomes.

Another major issue is that many homeowners never analyze how their mortgage fits into their broader financial plan. They may contribute to retirement accounts, maintain checking and savings accounts, and pay bills regularly, but they often fail to view the mortgage strategically. A mortgage should not exist in isolation. It should be integrated into an overall plan involving cash flow management, investing, risk reduction, tax planning, and wealth-building objectives.

The emotional side of mortgage debt is also significant. Many homeowners underestimate the stress created by long-term financial obligations. Carrying large debt balances for decades can create anxiety, reduce flexibility, and increase fear during economic downturns. Job loss, illness, market changes, or unexpected expenses can become far more stressful when large monthly obligations remain fixed for years.

Reducing mortgage debt can provide emotional freedom in addition to financial benefits. Many homeowners experience a greater sense of security, confidence, and peace of mind as their debt declines. Lower obligations create flexibility. Financial flexibility allows individuals to change careers, pursue entrepreneurial opportunities, travel, spend more time with family, or retire earlier. Mortgage reduction is not just about numbers. It is about increasing life options.

At the same time, balance remains essential. Paying off a mortgage aggressively while neglecting retirement savings, emergency reserves, or investment opportunities can create other financial risks. Intelligent mortgage payoff strategies involve balancing debt reduction with overall financial stability. The goal is not reckless payoff behavior. The goal is optimized financial positioning.

One of the most powerful mindset shifts homeowners can make is moving from passive debt management to active financial strategy. Passive homeowners simply make required payments and hope everything works out over time. Strategic homeowners analyze options, evaluate opportunities, improve efficiency, and continuously optimize their financial position.

This book is designed to help readers become strategic homeowners. That means understanding not only mortgage mechanics but also human behavior, financial habits, long-term planning, and wealth acceleration principles. The process of becoming financially stronger often begins with awareness. Once people understand where their money is going and how debt truly functions, they begin seeing opportunities they previously overlooked.

Many people assume financial freedom requires extraordinary income, luck, or advanced investing knowledge. In reality, financial improvement often starts with mastering basic financial fundamentals consistently over long periods. Mortgage optimization is one of those foundational skills that can dramatically influence long-term wealth outcomes.

Every dollar saved in interest is a dollar that can potentially be redirected toward investments, savings, retirement, business opportunities, education, travel, or family goals. Mortgage efficiency creates financial leverage. The less money lost to unnecessary interest over time, the more financial resources become available for wealth creation.

Another reason this topic matters so much is that housing expenses often represent the largest monthly cost in a household budget. Even small improvements in mortgage efficiency can therefore produce substantial financial impact over decades. Reducing a thirty-year mortgage to twenty-two years or even fifteen years can dramatically alter a family's financial future.

The earlier homeowners begin implementing strategic mortgage payoff methods, the greater the long-term benefit becomes. Time amplifies financial decisions. Delaying action by five or ten years may cost tens of thousands of dollars in additional interest that could have been avoided through earlier optimization.

This does not mean homeowners should panic or become financially obsessive. Sustainable progress is far more important than perfection. Many successful mortgage payoff journeys begin with small adjustments that gradually build momentum over time. The key is consistency, awareness, and intentional action.

Throughout this series, you will learn that mortgage acceleration is not simply about eliminating debt as quickly as possible. It is about creating a stronger financial foundation while maintaining balance and flexibility. Different strategies work for different individuals depending on income, goals, risk tolerance, family structure, and investment priorities. Some people prioritize peace of mind and security by eliminating debt rapidly. Others prefer balancing mortgage reduction with investing and business growth. Neither approach is automatically right or wrong. Financial intelligence involves understanding the trade-offs and aligning decisions with long-term objectives.

In the chapters ahead, you will begin learning specific strategies for reducing mortgage timelines, lowering interest costs, improving cash flow, and building long-term wealth more efficiently. Some strategies are simple and easy to implement immediately. Others require more advanced planning and financial discipline. Together, they create a powerful framework for transforming the mortgage from a long-term burden into a controlled financial tool.

The first step toward financial acceleration is awareness. Once you understand the true cost of a mortgage and why so many people remain trapped in debt unnecessarily, you begin developing the mindset required to create meaningful financial change. Knowledge creates options, and options create freedom.

The good news is that you do not need to become wealthy overnight to improve your financial future. You simply need to become intentional. Small strategic decisions repeated consistently over time can completely reshape the trajectory of your financial life. Mortgage freedom is not reserved for the ultra-rich. It is often achieved by ordinary people who decide to manage their finances differently from the majority.

The journey begins with understanding. Once you fully understand how mortgage debt works and how much long-term interest impacts your financial future, you will never view your mortgage the same way again.

How One Couple Took Control of Their Mortgage and Changed Their Financial Future

Michael and Elena Ramirez sat quietly at the kitchen table late one evening after putting their two children to bed. The house was finally silent except for the hum of the refrigerator and the soft sound of rain tapping against the windows. Spread across the table were bills, bank statements, mortgage paperwork, and a small notebook Elena had started using to track their finances.

Michael leaned back in his chair and rubbed his forehead. "I don't understand how we work this hard and still feel stuck," he said quietly.

Elena looked down at the numbers in front of her. “We make decent money,” she replied. “But every month it feels like we’re just surviving.”

They had purchased their home seven years earlier. At the time, it felt like a major accomplishment. Michael worked as a project manager for a construction company, and Elena worked remotely in medical billing while raising their children. Together, they earned enough to qualify for the mortgage comfortably. Their lender assured them the payment was affordable and normal for a growing family.

At first, they felt proud every time they made a mortgage payment. Owning a home represented stability, success, and security. But over time, reality began setting in. Despite making payments for years, their mortgage balance barely seemed to move. Property taxes increased. Insurance premiums rose. Home repairs appeared unexpectedly. Credit card balances occasionally crept higher during difficult months.

One evening, Michael logged into their mortgage portal out of curiosity. He stared at the remaining balance in disbelief. After seven years of payments, they had barely reduced the principal.

"How is this possible?" he asked Elena. "We've paid this thing for years."

Elena walked over and looked at the screen. The number shocked her too. They had spent years making payments faithfully, yet most of the money had gone toward interest rather than reducing the loan itself. For the first time, they truly understood how mortgages worked. They realized they had been operating on autopilot financially.

That night changed something in both of them.

Instead of feeling defeated, they became determined to understand their finances more deeply. Elena started reading books about mortgages, budgeting, and wealth-building. Michael listened to financial podcasts during his commute. Slowly, they began identifying patterns in their spending habits and financial behavior.

The first thing they discovered was how much money quietly disappeared every month through small unnecessary expenses. Subscription services, impulse purchases, dining out multiple times per week, and convenience spending added up far more than they realized. None of the individual purchases seemed major, but together they consumed hundreds of dollars monthly.

Importantly, they did not want to live miserably. They still wanted family outings, vacations, birthday celebrations, and occasional dinners out. Their goal was not deprivation. Their goal was control.

They began making small strategic adjustments rather than extreme sacrifices. Michael started bringing lunch to work several days a week instead of buying expensive meals daily. Elena created grocery plans that reduced waste significantly. They canceled subscriptions they barely used. They refinized their car insurance. They became more intentional without becoming obsessive.

The savings were not dramatic at first, but they created something powerful: extra cash flow.

Instead of allowing the extra money to disappear, they directed a portion toward additional mortgage principal payments each month. At first it was only a few hundred dollars. But over time, those payments started making a noticeable impact.

Michael became fascinated by amortization schedules. He realized that every extra principal payment reduced future interest. The earlier the payment was made, the greater the long-term savings became.

"It's like we've been feeding the bank all these years without understanding the game," he told Elena one night.

For the first time, they felt like they were gaining momentum instead of simply surviving.

Then something unexpected happened. The emotional atmosphere in their household began changing too. Financial stress had quietly impacted their marriage for years. Money discussions often created tension, anxiety, or frustration. But now they felt united by a shared mission. Instead of avoiding financial conversations, they began having regular planning meetings together.

They tracked progress monthly. Each small reduction in the mortgage balance became motivating. Every thousand dollars of principal reduction felt like reclaiming a piece of their future.

A year later, Michael received a bonus at work. In the past, they probably would have spent most of it on upgrades, vacations, or miscellaneous purchases. This time, they paused and evaluated their options carefully.

They decided to split the bonus strategically. Part went into emergency savings. Part funded a modest family vacation. The remaining portion went directly toward the mortgage principal.

That single payment removed nearly an entire year from their mortgage schedule.

The realization stunned them.

"That one decision just saved us thousands in interest," Elena said.

Michael nodded. "And we still got to enjoy life." The experience reinforced an important lesson: financial progress did not require perfection. It required intentionality.

Over the next several years, they continued optimizing gradually. Elena started a small side business helping local medical offices organize billing systems remotely. Michael occasionally picked up consulting work on weekends. Instead of allowing the extra income to inflate their lifestyle, they used much of it strategically.

Their mortgage balance began shrinking faster than they ever imagined possible.

Friends and family sometimes questioned why they focused so much on reducing debt instead of buying newer cars or upgrading houses. But Michael and Elena had started thinking differently. They no longer viewed financial success as appearances. They viewed success as freedom.

By their fifteenth year in the home, something remarkable happened.

Their mortgage was completely paid off.

The moment felt surreal.

Elena cried quietly when they received the payoff confirmation letter. Michael placed the letter on the kitchen table where their financial transformation had first begun years earlier.

The emotional impact surprised them both. The absence of the mortgage payment created an entirely new level of peace and flexibility. Suddenly, thousands of dollars each month became available for investing, traveling, helping their children, and building long-term wealth.

But perhaps the greatest change was psychological.

They no longer felt trapped.

The family vacations became more enjoyable because they were no longer financed through stress. Retirement planning accelerated dramatically. Their investment accounts grew faster. Unexpected expenses no longer created panic. Michael eventually reduced his work hours to spend more time coaching his son's soccer team. Elena expanded her business because she finally had the confidence to take calculated risks.

Years later, they reflected on what truly changed their lives.

It was not a massive inheritance. It was not winning the lottery. It was not becoming ultra-rich overnight.

It was learning how to think strategically about money.

They realized that small consistent decisions, repeated over long periods, could completely reshape a family's future. The mortgage that once felt like a lifelong burden eventually became the catalyst that forced them to gain financial awareness, discipline, and confidence.

Most importantly, they learned that paying off a mortgage early was never just about the house.

It was about freedom.

Chapter 2

The Power of Cash Flow Management and Why Income Alone Does Not Create Financial Freedom

One of the greatest misconceptions in personal finance is the belief that high income automatically creates wealth and financial freedom. Many people assume that earning more money will solve most financial problems. While income certainly matters, income by itself does not guarantee stability, peace of mind, or long-term financial success. In reality, countless individuals with high salaries remain financially stressed, overwhelmed by debt, and trapped in cycles of constant financial pressure. At the same time, some individuals with moderate incomes quietly build substantial wealth through disciplined cash flow management and intentional financial behavior.

Understanding cash flow is one of the most important skills a homeowner can develop when attempting to pay off a mortgage faster without sacrificing quality of life. Cash flow refers to the movement of money into and out of your financial life. Positive cash flow occurs when income exceeds expenses. Negative cash flow occurs when expenses consume most or all incoming money. Mortgage acceleration becomes extremely difficult without consistent positive cash flow because there is little flexibility to direct additional money toward principal reduction.

Many homeowners focus almost entirely on increasing income while ignoring spending patterns, financial inefficiencies, and long-term habits. They may work harder, pursue promotions, start side businesses, or take on overtime shifts, but if spending rises alongside income, financial progress often remains limited. This phenomenon is commonly referred to as lifestyle inflation. As earnings increase, expenses increase as well. Larger homes, luxury vehicles, expensive vacations, upgraded electronics, dining out frequently, subscription services, and impulse spending gradually consume the additional income.

Lifestyle inflation is dangerous because it creates the illusion of financial success while quietly reducing long-term financial flexibility. Someone earning a very high income may still live paycheck to paycheck if obligations continue expanding. Mortgage payoff becomes increasingly difficult when most monthly income is already committed to maintaining an expensive lifestyle.

This is why cash flow management matters so much. Financial freedom is often less about how much money you make and more about how much money you keep and direct strategically. A homeowner who controls expenses intelligently can often accelerate mortgage payoff far more effectively than someone who earns significantly more but spends carelessly.

One of the first steps in improving cash flow is gaining awareness. Many people have no clear understanding of where their money actually goes each month. Small expenses accumulate quietly over time and become normalized. Daily coffee purchases, convenience spending, delivery services, unused memberships, frequent dining out, impulse online shopping, entertainment subscriptions, and recurring fees may individually appear harmless, but collectively they can consume enormous amounts of cash flow over the course of a year.

The goal is not to eliminate all enjoyment or become financially obsessive. Sustainable financial improvement rarely comes from extreme deprivation. Instead, the objective is intentional spending. Intentional spending means directing money toward things that genuinely improve life while reducing wasteful or unconscious spending that does not create meaningful long-term value.

Many homeowners are surprised when they conduct a detailed review of their monthly expenses for the first time. They often discover hundreds or even thousands of dollars leaking out through habits they barely notice. These financial leaks reduce flexibility and delay progress toward important goals such as mortgage reduction, investing, emergency savings, retirement preparation, or business development.

Cash flow management also involves understanding fixed versus variable expenses. Fixed expenses include obligations that remain relatively stable each month, such as mortgage payments, insurance, utilities, car payments, and loan obligations. Variable expenses fluctuate based on behavior and choices, including dining, entertainment, shopping, travel, and discretionary spending.

While some fixed expenses may eventually be optimized through refinancing, downsizing, or restructuring debt, variable expenses usually provide the fastest opportunity for immediate improvement. Small adjustments in daily financial behavior can free up substantial cash flow over time without dramatically impacting quality of life.

One powerful strategy homeowners use is automation. When extra mortgage payments are automated, financial progress becomes more consistent. Instead of relying on emotional motivation each month, homeowners create systems that automatically direct a portion of income toward mortgage principal reduction. Automation reduces decision fatigue and helps transform good financial intentions into long-term habits.

Another important concept is income diversification. Many financially successful individuals develop multiple income streams rather than relying entirely on one paycheck. Additional income does not necessarily require working endless hours or creating massive businesses. Small side projects, consulting work, freelancing, rental income, online businesses, or monetizing existing skills can create extra cash flow that accelerates financial progress dramatically.

One of the reasons additional income streams are so powerful is because they often feel psychologically different from primary income. Many people become more comfortable directing side income toward debt reduction or investing because they do not rely on it for basic living expenses. Even relatively modest side income can produce enormous long-term impact when applied consistently toward mortgage principal.

For example, an extra five hundred dollars monthly directed entirely toward mortgage reduction may eliminate years from a loan term while saving substantial interest costs. Over time, strategic use of additional income becomes a wealth acceleration tool rather than simply a way to increase spending.

However, income generation alone is not enough if financial discipline is absent. Many individuals increase earnings but simultaneously increase debt and lifestyle obligations. This creates ongoing dependency on maintaining high income levels simply to survive financially. True financial freedom often comes not from maximizing income alone but from reducing financial dependency and increasing flexibility.

Emergency savings also play a critical role in cash flow management. Homeowners without emergency reserves are often forced to rely on credit cards, personal loans, or high-interest debt when unexpected expenses arise. Medical bills, vehicle repairs, home maintenance issues, or temporary job interruptions can quickly create financial instability without adequate reserves.

Building emergency savings may initially seem to compete with aggressive mortgage payoff goals, but both objectives are important. A homeowner who aggressively pays down a mortgage while maintaining no liquidity may become financially vulnerable during emergencies. Balance remains essential. Strong financial positioning usually involves both reducing debt and maintaining accessible reserves.

Another key component of cash flow management is avoiding unnecessary consumer debt. High-interest debt such as credit cards can significantly delay mortgage payoff progress because interest payments consume valuable cash flow. Many homeowners unknowingly prioritize consumption over long-term financial growth by financing lifestyle purchases that depreciate quickly while carrying long-term liabilities.

Developing disciplined spending habits often requires behavioral change rather than mathematical knowledge alone. Emotional spending, stress spending, comparison spending, and reward spending are extremely common. Many people spend money not because they truly need something but because spending temporarily creates emotional comfort, excitement, or validation.

Social pressure also influences financial behavior heavily. Modern culture often encourages visible consumption and external displays of success. Expensive cars, luxury homes, vacations, designer products, and social media lifestyles create constant comparison pressure. Many individuals spend money attempting to appear financially successful while privately experiencing significant financial stress.

One of the most empowering financial decisions homeowners can make is shifting focus away from appearances and toward long-term freedom. Wealth-building frequently requires delayed gratification and independent thinking. Financially disciplined individuals often prioritize ownership, flexibility, investments, and cash flow over short-term image enhancement.

Another major advantage of improved cash flow management is reduced stress. Financial pressure affects relationships, mental health, physical health, sleep quality, and overall life satisfaction. Homeowners living with constant financial strain often feel trapped regardless of income level. Improving cash flow creates breathing room. Breathing room creates confidence, clarity, and opportunity.

When homeowners gain control over cash flow, they begin making decisions from a position of strength rather than survival. They can plan strategically, invest thoughtfully, weather emergencies more effectively, and pursue opportunities that may have previously seemed impossible.

Cash flow management also creates momentum. Small financial wins build confidence. As homeowners see mortgage balances decline faster, emergency savings grow, and debt obligations shrink, motivation increases naturally. Financial discipline becomes easier when progress becomes visible.

Importantly, mortgage acceleration should enhance life rather than destroy it. Extreme financial restriction often leads to burnout and unsustainable behavior. The objective is not to eliminate all enjoyment or become consumed by financial anxiety. The objective is to build systems that create long-term stability while still allowing life to be enjoyed along the way.

Many homeowners discover that intentional spending actually increases happiness rather than reducing it. Instead of mindless consumption, they begin prioritizing experiences, relationships, health, freedom, and meaningful goals. Financial awareness often shifts perspective from temporary gratification toward long-term fulfillment.

Another powerful aspect of cash flow optimization is time leverage. As debt obligations decline, monthly financial requirements decrease. Lower obligations increase freedom dramatically. Some individuals eventually gain the flexibility to reduce work hours, change careers, start businesses, travel more, spend additional time with family, or retire earlier because they reduced long-term liabilities strategically.

Financial freedom is not necessarily about becoming extraordinarily wealthy. Often, it is about reducing dependency on large monthly obligations and creating flexibility over how time is spent. Mortgage reduction plays a major role in that process because housing costs represent one of the largest financial burdens most people carry.

As you continue through this series, you will learn increasingly advanced strategies for improving cash flow, accelerating mortgage payoff, optimizing financial efficiency, and building long-term wealth. However, the foundation of all these strategies remains the same: intentional financial management.

People who consistently control cash flow tend to build wealth more effectively regardless of income level. Those who ignore cash flow often remain financially stressed regardless of how much money they earn. The difference usually comes down to awareness, discipline, and long-term strategy.

Mortgage freedom does not happen accidentally. It is usually the result of thousands of intentional financial decisions made consistently over time. The good news is that even small improvements can create enormous long-term impact when repeated consistently.

Once homeowners understand the power of cash flow management, they stop viewing money as something that simply comes and goes randomly. Instead, they begin treating money as a strategic tool capable of creating stability, flexibility, opportunity, and freedom.

That mindset shift changes everything.

How Cash Flow Discipline Changed Marcus Bennett's Entire Future

Marcus Bennett had everything most people believed should create financial success. At thirty-eight years old, he worked as a senior software engineer earning well over six figures annually. He owned a beautiful suburban home, drove a luxury SUV, took expensive vacations, and regularly upgraded electronics, furniture, and appliances. From the outside, his life looked impressive.

But privately, Marcus felt exhausted.

Every month seemed to disappear financially before he fully understood where the money went. Despite his high income, he carried large credit card balances, a substantial mortgage, vehicle payments, and constant financial pressure. Unexpected expenses created anxiety instead of inconvenience. He often wondered how someone earning so much money could still feel financially fragile.

One Friday afternoon, Marcus sat in heavy traffic leaving work when his phone buzzed with a fraud alert from his bank. His checking account balance had dropped dangerously low after several automatic payments processed simultaneously.

He felt a wave of panic.

"How is this possible again?" he muttered to himself.

That evening, Marcus opened his banking apps and began reviewing transactions more carefully than he ever had before. What he discovered shocked him.

Money leaked everywhere.

Food delivery several times weekly. Subscription services he barely used. Frequent online shopping purchases. Expensive gym memberships. Luxury coffee stops twice daily. High car payments. Impulse purchases after stressful workdays. Multiple streaming platforms. Weekend spending habits he barely remembered by Monday morning.

None of the expenses individually seemed catastrophic. Together, they created a financial machine constantly consuming his income.

For the first time, Marcus realized he had confused income with wealth.

The following weekend, he sat down with a notebook and wrote out every recurring expense in his life. The numbers were uncomfortable to face, but they also created clarity. He realized that while he earned an excellent income, his lifestyle required nearly all of it.

That realization changed something mentally.

Marcus decided he no longer wanted to feel trapped by his own success.

Importantly, he did not want to become miserable or eliminate all enjoyment. He simply wanted control.

Instead of making extreme changes immediately, he focused on small strategic adjustments. He reduced food delivery dramatically and began cooking more meals at home. He canceled subscriptions he barely used. He refinanced his auto loan to reduce monthly obligations. He stopped impulse shopping late at night after stressful workdays.

Within a few months, his cash flow improved significantly.

For the first time in years, he had extra money remaining at the end of the month.

At first, Marcus considered upgrading parts of his lifestyle again. But something stopped him. He remembered the stress of feeling financially trapped despite earning so much money.

Instead, he made a different decision.

He began sending extra principal payments toward his mortgage every month.

At first the payments were small. But Marcus became fascinated watching the principal balance decline faster than before. He discovered online mortgage calculators and began experimenting with different payoff scenarios.

The results amazed him.

Small additional principal payments dramatically reduced future interest costs. By consistently adding extra money toward the mortgage, he could potentially eliminate years from the loan.

For the first time, Marcus felt like his income was creating actual progress instead of simply supporting consumption.

Then another opportunity appeared.

A former coworker asked Marcus to help with a freelance software project during evenings and weekends. In the past, Marcus likely would have used the extra money for luxury purchases or travel upgrades. This time, he treated the income differently.

He created a rule for himself: all freelance income would go directly toward wealth-building.

Some went into investments. Some strengthened emergency savings. Much of it went toward mortgage principal reduction.

Over time, the mortgage balance started falling noticeably faster.

But the biggest transformation was psychological.

Marcus no longer felt controlled by money.

As his financial obligations decreased, his confidence increased. He slept better. He stopped checking his bank balance anxiously every few days. Unexpected expenses no longer triggered panic. He realized that financial peace came not from appearing wealthy but from building stability and flexibility.

A year later, Marcus received a major promotion at work with another significant salary increase.

This time, instead of dramatically upgrading his lifestyle, he increased his mortgage payoff strategy further.

Friends questioned why he still drove the same vehicle or lived relatively modestly compared to others in his income bracket. Marcus simply smiled.

They did not understand what he understood now.

Freedom was more valuable than appearances. As the years passed, Marcus continued balancing enjoyment with intentionality. He still traveled. He still enjoyed hobbies. He still spent money on experiences he valued. But spending became conscious rather than automatic.

By his mid-forties, Marcus had eliminated his mortgage entirely.

The day he made the final payment felt surreal. He sat quietly in his living room staring at the confirmation statement on his laptop. The house around him suddenly felt different—not because the structure had changed, but because the financial burden attached to it had disappeared.

For the first time since becoming an adult, he truly felt financially free.

The impact on his life was enormous.

Without a mortgage payment, Marcus dramatically increased investments and retirement contributions. He eventually reduced his corporate workload and transitioned into consulting projects he genuinely enjoyed. He traveled more without financial guilt. He spent more time with family. Most importantly, he no longer felt dependent on maintaining an exhausting work pace simply to survive financially.

One evening, Marcus met an old colleague for dinner. The colleague earned even more money than Marcus but constantly complained about stress, bills, debt, and financial pressure.

At one point he asked, "How do you always seem so relaxed financially?"

Marcus paused for a moment before answering.

"I stopped trying to look wealthy," he said. "And started trying to become free."

The statement stayed with his colleague long after the dinner ended.

Marcus eventually realized that paying off the mortgage had not simply changed his finances. It had changed his relationship with money itself.

He no longer viewed income as something to consume immediately. He viewed money as a tool capable of creating flexibility, peace, security, and long-term opportunity.

Most importantly, he learned that financial freedom rarely depends on how much money enters your life.

It depends on how intentionally you manage what stays.

One evening, Marcus met an old colleague for dinner. The colleague earned even more money than Marcus but constantly complained about stress, bills, debt, and financial pressure.

At one point he asked, "How do you always seem so relaxed financially?"

Marcus paused for a moment before answering.

"I stopped trying to look wealthy," he said. "And started trying to become free."

The statement stayed with his colleague long after the dinner ended.

Marcus eventually realized that paying off the mortgage had not simply changed his finances. It had changed his relationship with money itself.

He no longer viewed income as something to consume immediately. He viewed money as a tool capable of creating flexibility, peace, security, and long-term opportunity.

Most importantly, he learned that financial freedom rarely depends on how much money enters your life.

It depends on how intentionally you manage what stays.

Chapter 3

Building a Mortgage Payoff Mindset Without Sacrificing Your Quality of Life

One of the most important steps in paying off a mortgage faster is developing the right mindset. Strategies matter, numbers matter, and income matters, but mindset is what determines whether a homeowner follows through consistently over time. Many people begin with excitement when they first decide to pay off their mortgage early, but they lose motivation when progress feels slow, life becomes busy, or unexpected expenses interrupt the plan. A strong mortgage payoff mindset helps homeowners stay focused without becoming extreme, discouraged, or financially unbalanced.

A mortgage payoff mindset does not mean becoming obsessed with debt elimination at the expense of everything else. It does not mean refusing to enjoy life, avoiding every vacation, eliminating every restaurant meal, or feeling guilty every time money is spent on something enjoyable. A healthy mortgage payoff mindset is built around intentionality. It means understanding where your money is going, deciding what truly matters, reducing waste, and using your financial resources in a way that supports both your present lifestyle and your future freedom. Many homeowners fail to make progress because they believe paying off a mortgage early requires painful sacrifice. They imagine years of restriction and frustration. This belief often prevents them from even starting. The truth is that mortgage acceleration does not have to feel like punishment. When done correctly, it can feel empowering. The goal is not to make life smaller. The goal is to make financial decisions smarter so your future becomes bigger.

The first part of building the right mindset is understanding that every financial decision has a future consequence. Money spent today may bring enjoyment, convenience, or comfort, but money directed toward principal reduction may reduce future interest, shorten the mortgage term, and increase long-term freedom. Neither choice is automatically wrong. The key is learning to make choices consciously instead of automatically.

A person who spends money intentionally can still enjoy life while making strong financial progress. For example, a family may choose to take one meaningful vacation each year instead of several expensive weekend trips they barely remember. Another homeowner may continue dining out occasionally but reduce unnecessary delivery expenses. Someone else may keep a hobby they love while cutting subscriptions, upgrades, and purchases that add little value. This is not deprivation. This is prioritization. Prioritization is one of the most powerful financial skills a homeowner can develop. Most people do not have unlimited income, which means they must choose where money goes. Without clear priorities, money often disappears into small habits, emotional spending, and convenience purchases. With clear priorities, money becomes a tool that supports the life you actually want.

A strong mortgage payoff mindset also requires separating wants from values. A want is something you may desire in the moment. A value is something that matters deeply over time. For example, a new luxury vehicle may be a want, while financial independence may be a value. A larger house may be a want, while peace of mind may be a value. Frequent impulse spending may satisfy short-term emotions, while mortgage freedom may support long-term security.

When homeowners connect mortgage payoff to their deeper values, the strategy becomes easier to maintain. Paying extra toward the mortgage is no longer just a financial transaction. It becomes an act of building security, protecting the family, creating options, reducing stress, and moving closer to freedom. This emotional connection is important because long-term financial goals require sustained motivation.

Another essential part of the mortgage payoff mindset is patience. Mortgage reduction rarely feels dramatic in the beginning. A homeowner may make extra payments for several months and feel disappointed that the balance has not fallen faster. This is especially common early in the process. However, mortgage acceleration works through consistency and compounding impact. Each extra principal payment reduces the balance, which reduces future interest, which allows future payments to become more effective. Momentum builds over time.

Many people give up too early because they expect immediate transformation. But mortgage payoff is not a quick sprint. It is a strategic campaign. The homeowner who stays consistent for years will often achieve results that seem impossible at the beginning. The key is trusting the process while periodically measuring progress.

Tracking progress can dramatically improve motivation. When homeowners see how much interest they have saved, how many months they have removed from the loan, or how much faster their principal is declining, they feel encouraged to continue. Progress tracking turns invisible financial improvement into visible motivation. It reminds homeowners that every additional dollar applied strategically is working for their future.

A mortgage payoff mindset also requires rejecting comparison. Comparison is one of the biggest enemies of financial progress. Many people make poor financial decisions because they compare their lifestyle to friends, relatives, neighbors, coworkers, or social media personalities. They upgrade cars, homes, clothing, vacations, and experiences to keep pace with appearances. Unfortunately, appearances rarely reveal financial reality. The person who looks successful may be deeply in debt, financially stressed, or completely dependent on maintaining a high income.

Financially successful homeowners learn to measure progress against their own goals, not against other people's lifestyles. They understand that freedom often looks ordinary from the outside. Driving a paid-off vehicle, living below one's means, avoiding unnecessary debt, and making extra mortgage payments may not look exciting to others, but these decisions can create extraordinary long-term results.

Another important mindset shift is understanding that the goal is control, not perfection. Many people abandon financial plans because they make one mistake and feel like they have failed completely. They overspend one month, miss an extra principal payment, or face an unexpected expense, and they allow discouragement to stop their progress. This is unnecessary. Real life is not perfectly predictable. A strong mortgage payoff plan must allow flexibility. There will be months when extra payments are smaller. There may be months when no extra payment is possible. There may be emergencies, repairs, medical expenses, job changes, or family needs that temporarily interrupt the plan. This does not mean the strategy has failed. It simply means the homeowner must adjust and continue. Long-term success comes from returning to the plan repeatedly, not from executing it perfectly every single month.

A healthy mortgage payoff mindset also includes liquidity awareness. Some homeowners become so passionate about paying off debt that they send every available dollar toward the mortgage while leaving themselves without emergency savings. While this may reduce principal faster, it can create financial vulnerability. If an emergency occurs, they may be forced to rely on credit cards or high-interest debt. That can undo progress quickly.

The wiser approach is balanced acceleration. Balanced acceleration means paying down the mortgage faster while still maintaining emergency savings, insurance protection, retirement contributions, and reasonable liquidity. This creates both progress and security. The purpose of mortgage payoff is to reduce stress, not create new forms of financial anxiety.

Another key principle is building habits instead of relying on willpower. Willpower is inconsistent. Some days people feel motivated, and other days they do not. Habits and systems are more reliable. Automating extra principal payments, scheduling monthly financial reviews, using separate savings accounts for goals, and creating spending rules can make mortgage acceleration easier. The less a homeowner depends on daily motivation, the more sustainable the plan becomes.

For example, a homeowner might decide that every tax refund, work bonus, commission check, or side-business profit will be split into three categories: savings, enjoyment, and mortgage principal reduction. This type of rule removes emotional decision-making. It allows the homeowner to enjoy life while still making consistent progress. Instead of debating every financial decision, the system guides the outcome.

A mortgage payoff mindset also involves redefining what luxury means. Many people think luxury is expensive products, upgraded homes, luxury cars, or visible status. But true luxury may be having a low monthly obligation, sleeping peacefully, taking time off without panic, helping children financially, retiring early, or having the freedom to choose work based on purpose instead of pressure. Mortgage reduction can create a deeper form of luxury: freedom from constant obligation.

This mindset shift can be life-changing. Once homeowners begin valuing freedom more than appearance, financial decisions become clearer. They may no longer feel tempted to impress others with purchases that delay their goals. They become more interested in owning their time than displaying their income. This is where true wealth acceleration begins.

Another important part of the mortgage payoff mindset is understanding the connection between today's discipline and tomorrow's options. Every extra principal payment is not just reducing debt. It is buying back future choices. It may shorten the number of years you must work under pressure. It may create room to invest more aggressively later. It may allow you to help family members, start a business, travel, or retire earlier. Debt reduction creates options, and options create freedom.

Homeowners should also recognize that mortgage payoff is not an all-or-nothing goal. Some people think they must either pay the mortgage off as fast as possible or make only the minimum payment. In reality, there are many levels between those extremes. A homeowner may choose to add $100 per month, make one extra payment per year, apply bonuses occasionally, use biweekly payments, or combine several methods gradually. Even moderate acceleration can produce meaningful results.

The best plan is usually the one the homeowner can sustain. An aggressive plan that fails after six months is often less effective than a moderate plan that continues for ten years. Sustainability should be treated as a core strategy, not a weakness. Paying off a mortgage faster while preserving quality of life requires a plan that fits real life.

Another helpful mindset is viewing the mortgage as a financial opponent that can be managed strategically. Instead of seeing the mortgage as a permanent burden, homeowners can see it as a challenge with rules, patterns, and opportunities. Amortization, interest, principal reduction, cash flow, refinancing, and payment timing all become tools to understand and use. This turns the homeowner from a passive borrower into an active strategist.

Becoming an active strategist builds confidence. Many people feel intimidated by mortgages because the numbers seem complicated. But once the basic concepts become clear, homeowners often realize they have more control than they thought. They can choose to make extra payments. They can analyze refinancing options. They can reduce unnecessary spending. They can increase income. They can protect liquidity. They can create a timeline. They can adjust when needed.

The mortgage payoff mindset also requires long-term vision. Without vision, extra payments can feel like lost spending money. With vision, those same payments feel like investments into future freedom. A homeowner with a clear vision may imagine the day the mortgage is gone, the monthly payment is eliminated, and cash flow is redirected toward wealth-building. That vision becomes fuel.

It is also important to involve the household when possible. If a spouse, partner, or family members are affected by the plan, shared understanding matters. Mortgage acceleration becomes easier when everyone knows the purpose and benefits. Instead of feeling like random restrictions, financial choices become part of a shared mission. Families can celebrate milestones together, such as reducing the balance by a certain amount or removing a year from the mortgage timeline.

Celebration is important because long-term goals need encouragement. Celebrating progress does not mean wasting money. It means recognizing success along the way. A small family dinner, a simple weekend activity, or even a printed progress chart can reinforce momentum. Mortgage payoff should not feel like endless punishment. It should feel like a journey with meaningful victories.

Another important concept is emotional resilience. Financial journeys often include setbacks. A homeowner may face unexpected repairs, temporary income loss, rising insurance costs, medical expenses, or family emergencies. These events can feel discouraging, but they do not erase progress. A strong mindset allows homeowners to pause, adjust, and resume. The ability to continue after setbacks is often more important than the original plan itself.

The ultimate purpose of developing a mortgage payoff mindset is to create alignment between money and life. Money should support your goals, values, security, and freedom. A mortgage should not silently control your future simply because no one taught you how to manage it strategically. Once your mindset changes, your financial behavior changes. Once your behavior changes, your results change.

Paying off a mortgage faster without sacrificing your lifestyle is not about living less. It is about living with greater purpose. It means choosing freedom over waste, strategy over autopilot, and long-term peace over short-term pressure. When homeowners develop this mindset, mortgage acceleration becomes more than a financial plan. It becomes a new way of thinking about ownership, discipline, and freedom.

The journey will not always be easy, but it can be deeply rewarding. Each extra payment, each intentional choice, each financial review, and each improvement in cash flow moves the homeowner closer to a more secure future. The mindset built along the way may become even more valuable than the mortgage payoff itself because it can influence every future financial decision. A paid-off home is powerful. But the disciplined, confident, strategic person who created that outcome is even more powerful. That person can build wealth, protect family, seize opportunities, and make decisions from strength. This is why mindset matters. It is the foundation beneath every successful mortgage payoff strategy.

How Daniel and Sofia Learned to Pay Down Their Mortgage Without Giving Up the Life They Loved

Daniel and Sofia Morales had always believed they were responsible with money. They paid their bills on time, had good credit, owned a comfortable home, and earned a steady household income. From the outside, their life looked stable and successful. They had two children, a nice neighborhood, two vehicles in the driveway, and enough income to enjoy restaurants, family trips, and weekend entertainment.

But every time Sofia looked at their mortgage statement, she felt uneasy.

They had purchased their home six years earlier with excitement and hope. At the time, the monthly payment seemed reasonable. Their lender explained the numbers, congratulated them at closing, and handed them the keys to what they believed would be their forever home. For the first few years, they felt proud to be homeowners.

Then one evening, while organizing paperwork, Sofia noticed how slowly their mortgage balance had declined. She called Daniel over and pointed to the statement.

"Look at this," she said. "We've been paying for six years, and the balance barely moved."

Daniel frowned. “That can’t be right.”

They pulled up the loan history online and reviewed the payments. Month after month, a large portion had gone to interest. The principal had moved, but not nearly as much as they expected.

For the first time, they realized that owning a home did not automatically mean they were building wealth quickly. Their mortgage was working exactly as designed, but they had never understood the design.

That night, they had a long conversation at the kitchen table. Daniel wanted to make aggressive extra payments immediately. Sofia was cautious. She worried about giving up vacations, fun activities with the kids, and the small pleasures that made life enjoyable.

“I don’t want to spend the next ten years feeling like we can’t live,” she said.

Daniel understood. “I don’t either. But I also don’t want to spend the next twenty-four years acting like this mortgage is just normal.”

They agreed on one principle: they would pursue mortgage freedom, but not through misery.

Their first step was awareness. For thirty days, they tracked every expense without judgment. The results surprised them. They were not wasting money in huge obvious ways. Instead, money was slipping away through convenience and habits. Takeout after busy workdays. Random online purchases. Extra subscriptions. Expensive weekend activities that did not always feel meaningful. Grocery waste. Last-minute spending because they failed to plan.

Sofia looked at the totals and laughed softly. "We don't need to suffer. We just need to stop being careless."

That became their new motto.

They created a monthly plan that protected what mattered most. They kept one family outing each month. They kept their annual summer trip, but reduced unnecessary upgrades. They continued date nights, but made them more intentional. Instead of spending randomly every weekend, they planned experiences they truly valued.

Then they created a mortgage freedom account. Every month, money saved from reduced waste went into that account first. At the end of the month, they sent it as an extra principal payment. The first payment was only $350.

Daniel felt slightly disappointed. "That doesn't seem like

much."

But Sofia had already entered the numbers into a mortgage calculator. "It matters more than you think," she said. "If we keep doing this, we could cut years off the loan."

That small win changed their attitude.

The next month, they found another $420. The month after that, Daniel received overtime pay and they added more. Instead of feeling deprived, they felt excited. Every extra payment became proof that they were taking control.

They printed a simple mortgage payoff chart and placed it inside a cabinet door where only they would see it. Each time their balance dropped by another milestone, they marked it. The chart became a private symbol of progress.

Their friends, however, did not always understand the change.

One Saturday, a couple they knew invited them on an expensive last-minute weekend trip. In the past, Daniel and Sofia would have said yes immediately and put most of the cost on a credit card. This time, they paused. They had already planned a family beach trip for later that year and did not want to interrupt their mortgage plan. They politely declined. Later that night, Daniel admitted he felt strange. "I don't want people to think we're broke."

Sofia looked at him and smiled. "We're not broke. We're choosing freedom."

That sentence stayed with Daniel.

Over the next year, their mindset continued changing. They stopped comparing their lifestyle to others. They stopped feeling pressured to upgrade things that still worked. They stopped believing that success had to be visible. Quietly, their financial life became stronger.

They built emergency savings. They paid off a small credit card balance. They continued making extra principal payments. They still enjoyed life, but now their spending matched their values.

The children even became part of the journey in a simple way. Daniel and Sofia explained that the family was working toward owning the home completely one day. They did not overwhelm the kids with details, but they taught them that money choices mattered. Instead of buying everything impulsively, they talked about saving for things that mattered.

One evening, their daughter asked, "When the house is paid off, does that mean we get to keep more of our money?" Daniel smiled. "Exactly."

"What will we do with it?"

Sofia answered, "We'll have more choices."

That became the deeper purpose behind everything.

A few years later, Daniel received a promotion. Their income increased significantly, but they made a decision before the first larger paycheck arrived. Half of the raise would go toward lifestyle improvements and family enjoyment. The other half would go toward mortgage principal.

This allowed them to enjoy progress without letting lifestyle inflation consume everything. They upgraded a few things that truly improved their life, but they also accelerated their payoff plan dramatically.

The mortgage balance began falling faster.

With every passing year, their confidence grew. They were no longer passive borrowers. They understood their loan. They understood their cash flow. They understood their priorities.

There were setbacks too. One year, the air conditioning system failed and cost thousands to replace. For several months, they paused extra mortgage payments to rebuild savings. In the past, that kind of interruption might have made them feel like failures. But now they saw it differently.

"This is why we kept emergency savings," Sofia said. "The plan is still working."

After the savings account recovered, they resumed extra payments.

This flexibility helped them stay committed. They were not following a rigid plan that broke under pressure. They were following a sustainable strategy that could adjust with life.

By the time they reached year fourteen in the home, they had cut their projected mortgage timeline dramatically. What once looked like a thirty-year obligation was now on track to disappear much earlier. Their financial stress had decreased. Their marriage felt stronger. Their children had watched them model discipline and balance.

One evening, Daniel and Sofia sat on the back patio after dinner. The kids were playing inside, and the sun was setting behind the fence.

Daniel looked around the yard and said, "I used to think paying off the mortgage meant giving everything up."

Sofia nodded. "I did too. But we didn't give up our life. We just stopped giving our money away without thinking."

That was the truth. They still celebrated birthdays. They still traveled. They still enjoyed dinners, holidays, and family memories. But they no longer allowed unconscious spending to delay their freedom.

Years later, when they finally made their last mortgage payment, the celebration was simple. They cooked dinner at home, invited close family, and placed the payoff letter in a frame. Their children cheered when Daniel announced that the house officially belonged to them.

Sofia cried as she looked around the room. The house had always been theirs emotionally, but now it was theirs financially too.

The freedom felt different than they expected. It was not loud or flashy. It was peaceful.

The next month, when no mortgage payment left their bank account, the reality fully hit them. Their cash flow changed instantly. They increased investments, helped their children with education savings, and created a travel fund without guilt. They had more options than ever before.

Daniel eventually told a younger coworker about the experience. The coworker asked, "Was it worth all the sacrifice?" Daniel smiled because he understood the question. Years earlier, he might have asked the same thing.

"It wasn't really sacrifice," he said. "It was alignment. We kept what mattered and cut what didn't. That's what gave us freedom."

The coworker nodded slowly, but Daniel knew the lesson would only fully make sense when experienced personally.

Daniel and Sofia's story was not about extreme wealth, perfect decisions, or overnight transformation. It was about a mindset shift. They stopped letting money drift away without purpose. They stopped trying to impress others. They stopped assuming a thirty-year mortgage had to last thirty years.

They chose freedom over appearances.

And by doing so, they discovered that the path to mortgage freedom did not require giving up the life they loved.

It required finally using their money to protect it.

Chapter 4

Creating Your First Mortgage Payoff Action Plan Step by Step

One of the biggest reasons homeowners fail to pay off their mortgage faster is not because they lack income, intelligence, or motivation. It is because they lack a clear action plan. Many people understand they would like to become debt-free earlier, but they never organize a structured strategy that turns the goal into measurable action. Without a plan, mortgage payoff remains a vague dream rather than a realistic financial objective.

Creating a mortgage payoff action plan is important because goals without structure rarely produce consistent results. A homeowner may occasionally make extra payments when money is available, but inconsistent action often leads to slow progress and reduced motivation. A well-designed plan transforms mortgage reduction from random behavior into an intentional financial system.

The first step in creating a mortgage payoff plan is understanding your current mortgage completely. Many homeowners know only the monthly payment amount but lack deeper knowledge about the loan itself. Before building a strategy, you must know the original loan amount, current balance, interest rate, remaining term, monthly payment breakdown, escrow structure, and whether any prepayment penalties exist.

Fortunately, most standard residential mortgages today allow extra principal payments without penalties. Still, homeowners should verify this directly with the lender or loan servicer. Understanding the loan structure removes uncertainty and creates clarity about what strategies are available.

One of the most powerful tools a homeowner can review is the amortization schedule. This schedule shows how each monthly payment is divided between principal and interest over the life of the loan. Seeing the numbers visually often creates urgency because borrowers realize how much future interest remains if no additional action is taken.

The amortization schedule also reveals where the greatest opportunities exist. In the early years of a mortgage, interest consumes a large percentage of each payment. This means extra principal payments made early in the loan term can produce significant long-term savings. The sooner a homeowner begins applying additional money toward principal reduction, the more effective the strategy becomes. After understanding the mortgage structure, the next step is identifying financial goals. Some homeowners want to eliminate the mortgage entirely as fast as possible. Others want to reduce the term moderately while balancing investing, retirement savings, or business growth. Some prioritize lower financial stress and peace of mind, while others focus primarily on maximizing long-term net worth.

There is no universal perfect strategy. The best mortgage payoff plan aligns with the homeowner's financial goals, personality, risk tolerance, family needs, and lifestyle preferences. A strategy that creates constant stress and frustration may not be sustainable long term. A balanced strategy that can be maintained consistently often produces better overall outcomes.

The next major step is analyzing cash flow honestly. Mortgage acceleration requires available cash flow. Without positive monthly cash flow, extra payments become difficult to sustain. This does not necessarily mean a homeowner must earn dramatically more money immediately. Often, the solution begins with improving awareness of spending habits and financial inefficiencies.

A homeowner creating a mortgage payoff plan should carefully review monthly expenses. The objective is not extreme deprivation but intentionality. Many people discover that hundreds of dollars quietly disappear each month through convenience spending, subscriptions, impulse purchases, dining out, unused memberships, delivery services, and financial habits that provide little long-term value.

Even relatively small improvements in spending efficiency can create meaningful mortgage acceleration opportunities. An extra two hundred dollars monthly directed toward principal may remove years from a mortgage timeline over time. The key is consistency rather than dramatic temporary sacrifices.

Once available cash flow is identified, homeowners should decide how aggressive they want the plan to be. Some choose fixed monthly extra payments. Others prefer percentage-based systems, such as directing a percentage of bonuses, commissions, or side income toward mortgage reduction. Some use hybrid approaches that combine multiple methods.

Consistency matters more than perfection. A homeowner who reliably adds a modest amount monthly often outperforms someone who attempts extremely aggressive payments briefly but eventually burns out or abandons the plan. Sustainable momentum is one of the most important factors in long-term mortgage acceleration success.

Automation can significantly improve consistency. When extra principal payments occur automatically, the homeowner removes emotional decision-making from the process. Automation transforms mortgage acceleration into a habit rather than a monthly debate. Many financially successful individuals use automation because systems tend to outperform willpower over long periods.

For example, a homeowner may set up automatic biweekly payments or schedule an automatic extra principal transfer every payday. Even small automated contributions can compound into substantial results over time. Automation also reduces the temptation to spend extra cash flow impulsively elsewhere.

Emergency savings must also be incorporated into the action plan. One of the biggest mistakes homeowners make is directing every available dollar toward the mortgage while neglecting liquidity. Financial emergencies are inevitable. Vehicle repairs, medical expenses, job interruptions, home maintenance, or unexpected family needs can quickly create financial stress.

A balanced mortgage payoff plan includes emergency reserves alongside debt reduction. Without savings, homeowners may become dependent on credit cards or personal loans during emergencies, which can reverse mortgage payoff progress quickly. Stability and flexibility are essential components of intelligent financial planning. Another important element is setting measurable milestones. Long-term financial goals can feel overwhelming if progress feels invisible. Breaking the journey into smaller milestones improves motivation dramatically. A homeowner may celebrate reducing the balance below certain thresholds, eliminating a full year from the loan term, or reaching specific equity milestones.

Progress tracking helps maintain momentum. Many homeowners lose motivation because they focus only on the distant final goal instead of recognizing ongoing progress. Tracking interest savings, reduced payoff timelines, and increasing equity can make the process feel rewarding and encouraging.

Mindset also plays a major role in sustaining the action plan. Mortgage acceleration should not become emotionally unhealthy or obsessive. Some homeowners become so focused on debt reduction that they eliminate all enjoyment, avoid all discretionary spending, and create unnecessary stress within the household. This often leads to burnout and resentment.

The healthier approach is intentional balance. Homeowners can still enjoy vacations, hobbies, celebrations, and meaningful experiences while pursuing mortgage freedom strategically. The objective is not to eliminate life enjoyment.

The objective is to reduce waste and align spending with long-term priorities.

A mortgage payoff plan should also include flexibility. Life circumstances change. Income fluctuates. Expenses rise unexpectedly. Children grow older. Careers evolve. Economic conditions shift. A rigid financial plan that cannot adapt may collapse during difficult periods. Flexible strategies allow homeowners to adjust temporarily without abandoning the overall mission.

For example, during strong financial periods, extra payments may increase significantly. During difficult months, the homeowner may reduce extra payments temporarily while maintaining stability. Long-term consistency matters more than short-term intensity.

Homeowners should also think strategically about additional income opportunities. Extra income streams can accelerate mortgage payoff dramatically when applied intentionally. Side businesses, freelance work, rental income, consulting, commissions, seasonal work, or monetizing skills may create substantial additional principal reduction opportunities over time.

Importantly, not every dollar of additional income must go toward the mortgage. A balanced approach often works best.

Some homeowners divide extra income among savings, investing, enjoyment, and mortgage reduction. This prevents the process from feeling emotionally restrictive while still accelerating financial progress significantly.

Another critical component of the mortgage payoff plan is avoiding new unnecessary debt. Mortgage acceleration becomes difficult when homeowners simultaneously accumulate additional consumer debt through vehicles, credit cards, personal loans, or luxury financing. Long-term financial freedom requires controlling liabilities overall, not just reducing one loan while increasing others.

This does not mean avoiding every purchase or living fearfully. It simply means evaluating whether new obligations support or delay long-term goals. Financial discipline is often about asking whether today's decision strengthens or weakens future flexibility.

A strong mortgage payoff plan also includes periodic reviews. Financial strategies should not remain completely static for decades. Interest rates change. Income changes. Investment opportunities change. Tax situations evolve. Homeowners should periodically review whether their current approach still aligns with their goals and circumstances.

Some homeowners eventually decide to refinance strategically. Others may shift focus toward investing after reaching certain equity levels. Some accelerate more aggressively after children leave home or after other debts are eliminated. Financial planning is dynamic rather than fixed.

Another important factor is emotional motivation. Mortgage payoff becomes easier when homeowners connect the goal to meaningful life outcomes. Paying off a mortgage is not simply about numbers on a spreadsheet. It may represent reduced stress, earlier retirement, greater security, freedom to travel, more family time, entrepreneurial flexibility, or the ability to help future generations financially.

When the emotional purpose becomes clear, consistency improves naturally. Homeowners stop viewing extra payments as "losing money" and begin seeing them as purchasing future freedom. That perspective shift changes behavior dramatically.

One effective exercise is visualizing life after the mortgage is gone. Imagine the monthly cash flow no longer required for housing debt. Imagine redirecting those funds toward investing, travel, family support, charitable giving, or lifestyle flexibility. This vision can create powerful long-term motivation.

Homeowners should also remember that mortgage payoff is not a competition. Every financial journey is different. Some individuals prioritize aggressive debt elimination. Others balance investing heavily alongside moderate mortgage reduction. Comparison often creates unnecessary pressure and poor decision-making. The best strategy is the one aligned with your own values and goals.

Importantly, homeowners should not underestimate the psychological benefits of reducing debt. Lower obligations create emotional breathing room. Financial resilience increases confidence. Reduced debt often improves sleep, relationships, career flexibility, and overall peace of mind. Mortgage payoff is not just mathematical. It is deeply connected to quality of life.

The process of creating and following a mortgage payoff plan also builds broader financial skills. Budgeting, cash flow awareness, discipline, strategic thinking, and long-term planning become habits that improve every area of financial life. The homeowner who successfully manages mortgage acceleration often becomes stronger financially overall.

One of the most empowering realizations homeowners experience is understanding that even small actions matter. Many people delay starting because they believe they cannot contribute enough to make a difference. But mortgage acceleration works through accumulation. Small extra payments repeated consistently create major long-term impact. A hundred dollars monthly may not seem life-changing immediately. But over years, combined with reduced interest accumulation, that consistency can save substantial money and eliminate years of payments. Time magnifies disciplined action.

Ultimately, the purpose of the mortgage payoff action plan is not simply eliminating debt faster. The deeper purpose is creating intentional financial control. Homeowners who actively manage their mortgage rather than passively accepting the original schedule gain flexibility, confidence, and opportunity.

The mortgage no longer becomes something happening to them. It becomes something they are strategically managing.

That shift changes everything.

How Small Extra Payments Can Save Years and Tens of Thousands of Dollars

Let's look at a realistic mortgage scenario to understand how powerful small extra principal payments can become over time.

Original Mortgage Scenario

- Loan Amount: $400,000
- Interest Rate: 7.00% fixed
- Loan Term: 30 years
- Monthly Principal & Interest Payment: Approximately $2,661
- Total Payments Over 30 Years: Approximately $958,000
- Total Interest Paid: Approximately $558,000

Most homeowners focus only on the $2,661 monthly payment. However, the true long-term cost of the loan is the total repayment amount, which in this case is nearly $958,000. That means the homeowner pays approximately $558,000 in interest alone over the life of the mortgage.

Now let's examine what happens when the homeowner starts making extra principal payments.

Example 1: Adding an Extra $200 Per Month

New Monthly Payment

- Original Payment: $2,661

- Extra Principal Payment: $200
- Total Monthly Payment: $2,861

Results

- Mortgage Payoff Time Reduced From 30 Years to Approximately 24 Years and 8 Months
- Time Saved: About 5 Years and 4 Months
- Total Interest Saved: Approximately $121,000

This means that by consistently adding just $200 monthly, the homeowner saves over five years of payments and more than $120,000 in interest.

That is the power of reducing principal early.

Example 2: Adding an Extra $500 Per Month

New Monthly Payment

- Original Payment: $2,661
- Extra Principal Payment: $500
- Total Monthly Payment: $3,161

Results

- Mortgage Payoff Time Reduced From 30 Years to Approximately 20 Years and 10 Months
- Time Saved: More Than 9 Years
- Total Interest Saved: Approximately $224,000

An extra $500 monthly removes nearly a decade from the mortgage timeline and saves well over two hundred thousand dollars in interest.

Example 3: One Extra Mortgage Payment Per Year

Another popular strategy is making one extra mortgage payment annually.

Monthly Equivalent

- Monthly Payment: $2,661
- One Extra Annual Payment: $2,661 per year

Results

- Mortgage Payoff Reduced From 30 Years to Approximately 24 Years
- Time Saved: About 6 Years

- Interest Saved: Approximately $135,000

This strategy alone can dramatically reduce long-term debt without requiring massive lifestyle changes.

Why These Numbers Matter

Most people underestimate how much interest compounds over time. The earlier extra payments are applied, the more future interest disappears. Every additional principal payment reduces the balance immediately, which reduces future interest calculations every month afterward.

This creates a compounding effect working in the homeowner's favor instead of the lender's favor.

Important Lesson

The key takeaway is this:

You do not need to completely change your life overnight to make major financial progress.

Small, consistent extra payments made strategically over time can:

- Remove years from your mortgage
- Save hundreds of thousands in interest

- Increase equity faster
- Reduce financial stress
- Create long-term freedom sooner

Mortgage acceleration is not about perfection.

It is about consistency.

Chapter 5

The Biweekly Payment Strategy and How Timing Alone Can Save You Thousands

One of the simplest yet most powerful mortgage acceleration strategies available to homeowners is the biweekly payment method. Unlike complicated financial systems that require major lifestyle changes, advanced investing knowledge, or large amounts of extra income, the biweekly strategy works primarily through payment timing and consistency. Many homeowners are surprised to learn that simply adjusting when payments are made can potentially save tens of thousands of dollars in interest and remove years from a mortgage term.

The reason this strategy is so effective is because it quietly increases the amount paid toward the mortgage each year without requiring dramatic financial sacrifice. Instead of making one full monthly mortgage payment twelve times per year, the homeowner makes half of the monthly payment every two weeks. Because there are fifty-two weeks in a year, this results in twenty-six half-payments annually, which equals thirteen full mortgage payments instead of twelve. That extra annual payment goes primarily toward principal reduction, especially when structured correctly. Over time, this additional principal reduction weakens future interest accumulation and accelerates the amortization process significantly.

At first glance, the difference may appear small. Many homeowners initially think, "How can one extra payment per year really matter that much?" But mortgage mathematics magnifies consistent extra principal payments dramatically over long periods. Because mortgages are heavily front-loaded with interest, reducing the balance earlier creates a cascading effect that lowers future interest charges month after month and year after year.

Another reason the biweekly strategy works well is because it aligns naturally with the pay schedules of many workers. Many employees receive paychecks every two weeks, making the biweekly mortgage structure feel psychologically manageable. Instead of trying to come up with one large payment monthly, homeowners spread the obligation across smaller, more frequent payments that often feel easier to budget.

This psychological advantage matters more than many people realize. Financial strategies are most effective when they are sustainable. A homeowner may understand the value of making large extra payments, but if the strategy creates constant stress or feels difficult to maintain, consistency often disappears. The biweekly method works because it integrates smoothly into everyday financial life.

One of the major benefits of the biweekly strategy is that it creates automation and momentum without requiring extreme discipline every month. Once the system is established, the homeowner continues making progress steadily. Mortgage reduction becomes systematic rather than emotional.

Many homeowners also appreciate that the strategy does not necessarily require sacrificing quality of life. In many cases, the half-payment every two weeks feels relatively manageable because the extra payment is spread throughout the year gradually rather than appearing as one large financial burden all at once.

However, homeowners should understand that not all biweekly programs are structured equally. Some mortgage servicers officially offer biweekly payment plans, while others do not. In some cases, third-party companies offer to manage biweekly payment systems for a fee. Homeowners should evaluate these services carefully because unnecessary fees can reduce the financial benefit.

Fortunately, many borrowers can create their own version of a biweekly strategy without paying outside companies. One common method involves simply making an extra monthly payment each year independently. Another approach involves dividing the monthly mortgage payment by twelve and adding that amount to each monthly payment, effectively creating the equivalent of one extra annual payment over time.

For example, if a monthly mortgage payment is $2,400, the homeowner could divide that amount by twelve, which equals $200. By adding an extra $200 monthly toward principal, the homeowner creates the equivalent of one extra mortgage payment annually without using a formal biweekly system.

This flexibility is important because every household manages cash flow differently. Some people prefer true biweekly scheduling. Others prefer monthly automation. The core principle is the same: increasing annual principal reduction consistently.

The biweekly strategy becomes especially powerful during the early years of a mortgage. Because interest consumes such a large percentage of payments initially, extra principal reductions made early can save substantial money over the life of the loan. Waiting ten or fifteen years to begin acceleration strategies often reduces the long-term impact significantly because much of the interest has already been paid.

Another major advantage of the biweekly strategy is that it builds equity faster. Equity represents ownership value in the property, calculated as the difference between the home's market value and the remaining loan balance. Faster principal reduction means faster equity growth.

Increased equity creates financial flexibility. Homeowners with higher equity positions often experience lower financial risk, stronger borrowing options if necessary, and greater protection during housing market fluctuations. Equity growth also improves long-term net worth and financial stability.

The emotional benefits of accelerated equity growth should not be underestimated either. Many homeowners feel trapped when large mortgage balances barely seem to decline year after year. The biweekly strategy creates visible progress more quickly, which increases motivation and confidence. Seeing the balance move faster reinforces positive financial behavior.

One important concept homeowners must understand is how interest accrues daily on many mortgage loans. When payments are made more frequently, principal may begin reducing earlier, slightly lowering the amount of interest accruing over time. While the biggest benefit still comes from the equivalent extra annual payment, payment timing itself can provide additional advantages depending on loan structure.

Another powerful aspect of the biweekly strategy is its simplicity. Many advanced financial systems fail because they are overly complicated. Complexity creates confusion, inconsistency, and frustration. The biweekly method succeeds partly because homeowners can understand it easily and implement it without advanced financial expertise.

Simplicity often wins in long-term financial planning because sustainable systems matter more than theoretical perfection. A homeowner who consistently follows a simple acceleration plan for fifteen years often achieves far greater results than someone who constantly changes complicated strategies without maintaining discipline.

Still, homeowners should avoid assuming the biweekly strategy alone solves every financial challenge. Mortgage acceleration must exist within a balanced overall financial plan. Emergency savings, retirement planning, insurance protection, cash flow stability, and debt management remain important. Paying down a mortgage aggressively while neglecting all other financial priorities can create unnecessary vulnerability.

Balance is especially important during uncertain economic periods. Job markets shift, medical emergencies occur, and unexpected expenses arise. A homeowner who sends every available dollar toward principal without maintaining liquidity may struggle during emergencies. Financial resilience requires both debt reduction and accessible reserves. Another common mistake homeowners make is forgetting to specify that extra funds should be applied directly toward principal reduction. Mortgage servicers sometimes apply additional funds differently unless instructions are clear. Homeowners should review statements carefully to ensure the strategy functions correctly.

Some homeowners choose to combine the biweekly strategy with other mortgage acceleration methods. For example, they may use biweekly payments consistently while also applying tax refunds, bonuses, commissions, or side-business income toward additional principal reductions periodically. Combining multiple moderate strategies often produces substantial long-term results without creating severe lifestyle pressure.

The biweekly strategy also highlights a larger financial principle: consistency matters more than intensity. Many people delay taking action because they feel unable to make dramatic changes immediately. But long-term financial success often comes from relatively small improvements repeated consistently over many years.

This principle applies far beyond mortgages. Retirement investing, business growth, health improvement, skill development, and wealth-building all benefit from consistent disciplined action over time. Small actions compounded through time create powerful outcomes.

Another important psychological advantage of the biweekly system is that it creates forward momentum automatically. Momentum matters because financial progress often feels slow initially. Many homeowners lose motivation when results are not immediately visible. The biweekly system helps maintain steady progress even during periods when motivation fluctuates.

Homeowners should also understand that mortgage acceleration creates opportunity cost reduction. Every dollar saved in interest becomes available for future investing, retirement savings, business development, family support, travel, or other financial goals. Reducing unnecessary interest improves long-term financial efficiency dramatically.

One of the most inspiring aspects of the biweekly strategy is that it proves financial freedom does not always require extreme wealth. Ordinary homeowners with average incomes can significantly improve their financial future simply through intentional systems and disciplined consistency. Financial improvement often depends more on behavior than income alone.

The biweekly strategy also changes how homeowners think about debt psychologically. Instead of viewing the mortgage as a fixed thirty-year obligation, they begin seeing it as something flexible and manageable. This shift in mindset creates empowerment. Homeowners stop feeling trapped by the original schedule and begin actively influencing the outcome.

Importantly, homeowners should remain patient during the process. Mortgage acceleration is gradual. The first few months may not feel dramatic. But over time, the compounding effect becomes increasingly powerful. Consistent extra payments reduce principal, which reduces future interest, which accelerates future payoff speed further. Momentum builds slowly at first, then more visibly later.

Some homeowners become discouraged because they expect instant transformation. But sustainable financial progress rarely happens overnight. Mortgage freedom is usually built through years of disciplined intentional action rather than one dramatic event.

Another benefit of the biweekly strategy is flexibility. If financial hardship occurs temporarily, homeowners may often return to standard monthly payment structures without permanently damaging long-term progress. This flexibility reduces psychological pressure and makes the strategy easier to sustain during real-life circumstances. As homeowners gain confidence, many eventually expand their financial planning beyond mortgage reduction alone. They begin investing more strategically, building additional income streams, strengthening savings, and improving long-term wealth creation. Mortgage acceleration often becomes the starting point for broader financial transformation.

The reason is simple: when people see themselves successfully controlling one major financial area, confidence expands into others. Financial discipline becomes part of identity rather than temporary behavior. The homeowner no longer feels powerless around money. They become proactive, intentional, and strategic.

Ultimately, the biweekly strategy teaches an extremely important lesson about wealth-building. Small adjustments applied consistently over time can create life-changing outcomes. Most people underestimate the power of timing, consistency, and compound impact because results seem small initially. But over years and decades, these systems become incredibly powerful.

A mortgage does not have to last thirty years simply because the original paperwork says so. Homeowners who understand timing and principal reduction can reshape the entire financial trajectory of the loan.

That realization creates possibility.

How a Biweekly Payment Strategy Can Save Thousands and Eliminate Years of Mortgage Payments

Let's look at a realistic example to understand how powerful the biweekly strategy can become over time.

Original Mortgage Scenario

- Loan Amount: $350,000
- Interest Rate: 6.75% fixed
- Loan Term: 30 years
- Monthly Principal & Interest Payment: Approximately $2,270
- Total Payments Over 30 Years: Approximately $817,200
- Total Interest Paid: Approximately $467,200

Most homeowners focus only on the monthly payment of $2,270. However, the long-term interest cost is enormous—over $467,000 in interest alone if only minimum payments are made for the full thirty years.

Now let's compare this to using a biweekly payment strategy.

Standard Monthly Payment Structure

- 12 Monthly Payments Per Year
- Annual Mortgage Payments: $2,270 × 12 = $27,240 annually

Biweekly Payment Structure

Instead of paying $2,270 once per month, the homeowner pays half every two weeks.

Biweekly Payment

- $2,270 ÷ 2 = $1,135 every two weeks

Because there are 26 biweekly periods per year:

- $1,135 × 26 = $29,510 annually

This equals the equivalent of 13 full mortgage payments instead of 12.

Extra Payment Generated Automatically

- Extra Annual Payment: Approximately $2,270 per year

Most importantly, this extra payment goes primarily toward principal reduction.

Results of the Biweekly Strategy

Mortgage Payoff Timeline

- Original Mortgage Term: 30 years
- New Estimated Payoff Time: Approximately 24 years and 3 months

Time Saved

- Approximately 5 years and 9 months removed from the mortgage

Interest Savings

- Estimated Interest Saved: Approximately $108,000

That means simply restructuring the payment timing and creating one extra annual payment saves over five years of mortgage payments and more than one hundred thousand dollars in interest.

Why This Works So Powerfully

The extra annual payment reduces principal earlier each year. Since future interest is calculated on the remaining balance, every principal reduction weakens future interest accumulation.

The earlier the balance declines, the less total interest the lender can charge over time.

This creates a compounding savings effect.

Even More Powerful Scenario

Now let's combine the biweekly strategy with a modest additional principal contribution.

Additional Extra Principal

- Extra Monthly Principal: $200

Combined Strategy Results

- Estimated Mortgage Payoff Time: Approximately 20 years and 8 months
- Total Time Saved: More than 9 years
- Estimated Interest Saved: Approximately $196,000

This example demonstrates how combining small consistent strategies can produce extraordinary long-term financial results.

Key Takeaway

The biweekly strategy proves an important principle:

You do not always need massive income increases or extreme lifestyle sacrifices to make major financial progress. Sometimes, changing the timing and consistency of payments alone can:

- Remove years from your mortgage
- Save six figures in interest
- Increase equity faster
- Reduce long-term financial stress
- Accelerate financial freedom dramatically

Small strategic adjustments become powerful when repeated consistently over time.

Chapter 6

Using Lump Sum Payments Strategically to Eliminate Years of Mortgage Debt

One of the fastest ways to accelerate mortgage payoff is through strategic lump sum principal payments. While small consistent extra payments create powerful long-term results, larger occasional principal reductions can dramatically transform the trajectory of a mortgage in a relatively short period of time. Many homeowners underestimate how impactful even one well-timed lump sum payment can become over the life of a loan.

A lump sum mortgage payment refers to any larger-than-normal amount applied directly toward reducing principal. These payments may come from tax refunds, work bonuses, commissions, inheritances, investment profits, side businesses, overtime income, legal settlements, business sales, or other financial windfalls. When used intentionally, lump sum payments can remove years from a mortgage schedule while saving tens or even hundreds of thousands of dollars in future interest. The reason lump sum payments are so effective is because they attack the principal balance directly and immediately. Since mortgage interest is calculated based on the remaining balance, every substantial principal reduction decreases future interest accumulation. The earlier the payment occurs in the life of the loan, the greater the long-term savings potential becomes.

Many homeowners initially assume they need enormous amounts of money to make meaningful progress. In reality, lump sum payments do not have to be massive to create noticeable impact. Even relatively modest annual contributions can significantly shorten mortgage timelines when applied consistently over time.

One important mindset shift homeowners must develop is learning to view windfalls strategically rather than emotionally. Most people instinctively spend unexpected money quickly because it feels separate from normal income. Tax refunds, bonuses, commissions, and gifts often trigger emotional spending behavior because the money feels like "extra money" rather than part of long-term financial planning.

This emotional reaction is understandable, but it can delay financial progress dramatically. Many individuals receive substantial windfalls throughout their lives yet remain financially stressed because the money disappears into temporary lifestyle upgrades, impulse purchases, vacations, or depreciating assets rather than strengthening long-term financial stability.

Financially disciplined homeowners approach windfalls differently. Instead of automatically spending all unexpected income, they evaluate how a portion could improve their long-term financial position. This does not necessarily mean eliminating all enjoyment. A balanced strategy often works best. Some homeowners divide windfalls intentionally between enjoyment, savings, investing, and mortgage reduction.

For example, a homeowner receiving a $10,000 work bonus may decide to allocate part toward a vacation or celebration while directing another portion toward mortgage principal. This balanced approach allows enjoyment without sacrificing long-term financial acceleration.

One of the biggest advantages of lump sum payments is that they can create immediate visible progress. Unlike small monthly additions that accumulate gradually, large principal reductions often produce dramatic balance decreases quickly. This can be highly motivating psychologically because homeowners see measurable change immediately.

Mortgage payoff journeys often become easier once momentum builds emotionally. When homeowners witness their balance declining faster, they feel more empowered and engaged financially. Motivation strengthens when progress becomes visible.

Another important concept homeowners should understand is the relationship between lump sum timing and interest savings. A $10,000 principal payment made during year three of a mortgage may save far more long-term interest than the same payment made during year twenty-five. Early principal reductions interrupt future interest accumulation for many additional years, amplifying the savings dramatically.

This is why starting early matters so much. Even homeowners unable to make enormous contributions initially can benefit significantly by applying smaller lump sums during the early stages of the mortgage. Time magnifies financial decisions.

Many homeowners use tax refunds strategically because refunds often arrive as predictable annual lump sums. Instead of viewing refunds purely as spending opportunities, some borrowers direct part or all of the refund toward principal reduction. Over multiple years, this strategy alone can remove significant time from the mortgage.

Work bonuses and commission income also create strong opportunities for acceleration. Because these payments are often separate from regular monthly budgeting, homeowners may feel more comfortable directing them toward long-term financial goals. Some individuals establish rules in advance, such as automatically sending fifty percent of all bonuses toward mortgage principal.

This type of system removes emotional decision-making and creates consistency. Financial systems often outperform motivation because they reduce impulsive behavior and simplify choices.

Side business income can also become an extraordinary mortgage acceleration tool. Many homeowners create additional income streams not necessarily to increase lifestyle spending but to improve long-term financial freedom. Freelancing, consulting, online businesses, rental income, coaching, tutoring, or monetizing skills can generate lump sum opportunities throughout the year.

Importantly, the purpose of additional income should not always be immediate consumption. When strategically applied toward principal reduction, side income can permanently reduce future financial obligations. Every extra dollar directed toward principal today may eliminate multiple future dollars of interest payments.

Another powerful strategy involves applying raises partially toward mortgage reduction instead of allowing lifestyle inflation to consume all income increases. Many individuals receive salary increases over time yet experience little improvement in financial freedom because expenses rise alongside earnings. Redirecting even part of income growth toward mortgage acceleration can produce enormous long-term benefits.

For example, if a homeowner receives a monthly raise of $800 after taxes, they may choose to direct $400 toward lifestyle improvements and $400 toward principal reduction. This balanced approach improves quality of life while simultaneously accelerating financial progress.

One critical issue homeowners must avoid is neglecting emergency savings while pursuing aggressive lump sum strategies. While principal reduction is valuable, maintaining liquidity remains essential. Unexpected emergencies can quickly create financial instability if all available cash has been tied up in home equity without accessible reserves.

Balanced financial planning requires both debt reduction and emergency preparedness. Homeowners should avoid becoming "house rich but cash poor." Financial flexibility matters as much as equity growth.

Another important consideration is opportunity cost. Some homeowners wonder whether extra money should go toward mortgage payoff or investing instead. The answer depends on multiple factors including interest rates, investment opportunities, risk tolerance, emotional preferences, tax considerations, and long-term goals.

For some individuals, reducing guaranteed mortgage interest expenses provides peace of mind and financial stability that outweighs potential investment returns. Others may prefer balancing mortgage reduction with aggressive investing strategies. Neither approach is universally correct. The key is making intentional informed decisions rather than defaulting into passive financial behavior.

Lump sum payments also reduce psychological stress significantly. Large debt balances often create emotional pressure even when monthly payments are manageable. Watching the principal decline more rapidly creates confidence, security, and a growing sense of control. Homeowners begin feeling less trapped by long-term obligations.

This emotional shift can influence many areas of life positively. Reduced financial stress often improves relationships, sleep quality, decision-making, career flexibility, and overall well-being. Mortgage reduction is not purely mathematical. It affects emotional freedom as well.

Another advantage of lump sum reduction is accelerated equity creation. Faster equity growth improves financial resilience and creates options. Homeowners with strong equity positions often feel more secure during economic downturns or housing market fluctuations because they owe significantly less relative to property value.

Increased equity may also create future opportunities if strategically needed. Homeowners with substantial equity may later leverage it responsibly for business opportunities, investments, education funding, or other wealth-building purposes. The key difference is that they control the debt rather than the debt controlling them.

One mistake some homeowners make is waiting for the "perfect" financial moment before starting lump sum strategies. They believe they must first earn significantly more money, eliminate every other expense, or achieve ideal financial conditions. Unfortunately, waiting often delays years of potential interest savings.

Progress usually begins with imperfect action. Small strategic lump sums applied consistently often outperform delayed perfection. A homeowner who applies several moderate lump sums over ten years may create extraordinary results even without dramatic income changes.

Another powerful strategy is applying debt snowball or debt avalanche principles before redirecting freed-up payments toward the mortgage. For example, once a vehicle loan or credit card is paid off, the former payment amount can be redirected toward mortgage principal. This creates increasing financial momentum over time.

Momentum matters enormously in financial behavior. As homeowners eliminate debts sequentially and redirect payments strategically, financial acceleration compounds. What begins as modest progress often becomes substantial later because cash flow continuously improves.

One reason lump sum payments feel so powerful psychologically is because they create visible ownership progress. Many homeowners spend years feeling like the bank owns most of the house. Each large principal reduction increases the homeowner's ownership percentage more rapidly, reinforcing the feeling of financial independence.

Homeowners should also remember that mortgage payoff is not necessarily all-or-nothing. Some individuals become discouraged because they cannot make massive lump sums immediately. But even moderate contributions matter. A few thousand dollars annually applied consistently can dramatically alter the life of a mortgage over decades.

Another important principle is intentional celebration. Financial progress should be recognized. When homeowners apply large lump sums successfully, acknowledging the achievement helps reinforce positive behavior. This does not require expensive celebrations. Simple recognition of progress strengthens motivation and commitment.

It is also important to communicate clearly with mortgage servicers to ensure lump sum payments apply directly toward principal reduction. Homeowners should verify payment processing carefully and review updated loan balances afterward.

Lump sum strategies also teach an important broader financial lesson: money can either disappear temporarily or create permanent improvement. A windfall spent impulsively may create short-term excitement but no lasting financial change. The same windfall applied strategically may reduce years of debt obligations permanently.

This realization changes the way many homeowners think about money. Instead of viewing financial windfalls as opportunities for consumption alone, they begin seeing them as tools for creating future freedom.

Ultimately, the purpose of strategic lump sum payments is not simply reducing a mortgage balance faster. The deeper purpose is reducing future obligations, increasing flexibility, and accelerating long-term financial independence.

Every large principal payment weakens future interest accumulation. Every reduced year of mortgage payments increases future cash flow freedom. Every strategic decision compounds over time.

The homeowner who understands this no longer sees windfalls as random spending money.

They see them as opportunities to buy back years of freedom.

How Strategic Lump Sum Payments Can Save Hundreds of Thousands of Dollars

Let's look at a realistic mortgage scenario to understand how powerful lump sum principal payments can become.

Original Mortgage Scenario

- Loan Amount: $500,000
- Interest Rate: 6.50% fixed
- Loan Term: 30 years
- Monthly Principal & Interest Payment: Approximately $3,160

- Total Payments Over 30 Years: Approximately $1,137,600
- Total Interest Paid: Approximately $637,600

Most homeowners focus on the $3,160 monthly payment. However, the long-term interest cost exceeds $637,000 over the life of the loan.

Now let's examine how strategic lump sum payments change the outcome.

Example 1: Applying a $10,000 Annual Lump Sum

Imagine the homeowner receives annual bonuses, tax refunds, commissions, or side-business income and applies $10,000 toward principal every year.

Annual Strategy

- Regular Mortgage Payment: $3,160 monthly
- Additional Lump Sum: $10,000 annually

Results

- Mortgage Payoff Time Reduced From 30 Years to Approximately 18 Years and 9 Months
- Time Saved: More Than 11 Years

- Estimated Interest Saved: Approximately $278,000

This means consistent annual lump sum payments can remove over a decade from the mortgage timeline while saving nearly three hundred thousand dollars in interest.

Example 2: One-Time $50,000 Lump Sum During Year 5

Now let's imagine the homeowner receives a large inheritance, investment profit, or business payout during year five and applies a one-time $50,000 principal reduction.

Results

- Mortgage Payoff Time Reduced From 30 Years to Approximately 24 Years and 4 Months
- Time Saved: About 5 Years and 8 Months
- Estimated Interest Saved: Approximately $163,000

One single lump sum payment created over five years of time savings and reduced future interest dramatically.

Example 3: Combining Monthly Extra Payments with Annual Lump Sums

Now let's combine strategies.

Combined Strategy

- Extra Monthly Principal Payment: $300
- Annual Lump Sum Payment: $5,000

Results

- Mortgage Payoff Time Reduced From 30 Years to Approximately 19 Years and 11 Months
- Total Time Saved: More Than 10 Years
- Estimated Interest Saved: Approximately $252,000

This example demonstrates how moderate consistent strategies combined together can create extraordinary long-term financial improvement.

Why Lump Sum Payments Are So Powerful

Mortgage interest compounds over time based on the remaining balance. Large principal reductions early in the loan dramatically weaken future interest accumulation.

Every dollar reducing principal today prevents future interest from being charged on that dollar for years or decades afterward.

This is why early action matters so much.

Key Lesson

You do not always need massive income increases to transform your financial future.

Strategic use of:

- Tax refunds
- Bonuses
- Side income
- Commission checks
- Investment profits
- Overtime income
- Inheritances
- Business income

can:

- Remove years from your mortgage
- Save hundreds of thousands in interest
- Increase equity rapidly

- Improve cash flow faster
- Reduce long-term financial stress dramatically

Lump sum payments are not just extra payments.

They are future freedom purchased early.

Chapter 7

Refinancing Strategically to Accelerate Mortgage Payoff and Reduce Long-Term Interest

Refinancing is one of the most misunderstood tools in mortgage management. Many homeowners view refinancing as something done only to lower monthly payments, while others avoid it completely because they assume refinancing always creates more debt or restarts the mortgage timeline unfairly. The truth is that refinancing can either become a powerful wealth-building strategy or an expensive financial mistake depending on how it is used.

Understanding how to refinance strategically is essential for homeowners who want to reduce long-term interest costs, improve cash flow, and potentially accelerate mortgage payoff significantly. Refinancing is not automatically good or bad. It is simply a financial tool. Like any tool, the outcome depends on the purpose, structure, timing, and execution.

At its core, refinancing means replacing an existing mortgage with a new loan. The new loan pays off the original mortgage, and the homeowner begins making payments under the new terms. These new terms may include a different interest rate, loan term, payment structure, or loan type.

One of the most common reasons homeowners refinance is to reduce interest rates. Even a relatively small decrease in mortgage interest can create enormous long-term savings over time. Because mortgages involve large balances over many years, small rate differences compound dramatically.

For example, reducing a mortgage rate from 7.00% to 5.75% may not initially appear life-changing monthly, but over decades it can save tens or even hundreds of thousands of dollars in interest. Many homeowners underestimate how powerful rate reductions become when multiplied across thirty years of payments.

However, refinancing solely for lower monthly payments can sometimes become dangerous if homeowners fail to understand amortization. One common mistake is repeatedly refinancing into new thirty-year mortgages while extending debt obligations far longer than necessary. Lower monthly payments may temporarily improve cash flow, but restarting the amortization schedule repeatedly can increase total long-term interest exposure substantially.

This happens because mortgages are heavily front-loaded with interest. Each time a homeowner refinances into a new long-term loan, they often restart the early interest-heavy portion of amortization. Without careful planning, the homeowner may unintentionally spend decades paying mostly interest repeatedly while building equity slowly.

This is why strategic refinancing requires looking beyond monthly payment amounts alone. Intelligent refinancing focuses on the overall financial picture, including total interest savings, remaining loan term, cash flow improvement, long-term goals, and future flexibility.

One of the most effective refinancing strategies involves reducing both the interest rate and the loan term simultaneously. For example, a homeowner with twenty-five years remaining on a thirty-year mortgage may refinance into a fifteen-year or twenty-year loan if financially manageable. This often dramatically accelerates principal reduction while lowering total interest costs substantially.

Shorter-term loans generally carry lower interest rates because lenders face reduced long-term risk exposure. As a result, homeowners may benefit from both lower rates and faster payoff structures simultaneously.

However, shorter-term refinancing also increases required monthly payments. Homeowners must evaluate cash flow carefully before choosing aggressive loan structures. Financial stress should not be ignored simply to accelerate payoff faster.

Sustainability matters.

Some homeowners choose a hybrid approach instead. They refinance into a new thirty-year loan with a lower rate to improve cash flow flexibility, then voluntarily continue making larger payments similar to the old payment amount. This allows them to accelerate payoff while still maintaining flexibility during emergencies or temporary financial setbacks.

Flexibility is valuable because life circumstances change. Income fluctuates. Expenses rise unexpectedly. Medical issues occur. Job transitions happen. A flexible loan structure can provide emotional and financial breathing room while still supporting long-term acceleration goals.

Another important refinancing strategy involves removing expensive mortgage insurance. Homeowners who originally purchased with smaller down payments may eventually refinance once sufficient equity exists, eliminating private mortgage insurance payments. Removing mortgage insurance can improve monthly cash flow significantly, allowing the homeowner to redirect those savings toward principal reduction or other financial goals.

Cash-out refinancing is another refinancing option homeowners sometimes use strategically. In a cash-out refinance, the homeowner borrows against accumulated home equity and receives cash at closing. While this increases the mortgage balance, it may create opportunities if used carefully and intelligently.

For example, some homeowners use cash-out refinancing to eliminate high-interest consumer debt, fund business opportunities, improve income-producing properties, or invest in long-term wealth-building projects. However, this strategy requires discipline because it converts equity into debt again. Poorly managed cash-out refinancing can delay financial freedom significantly if funds are spent irresponsibly.

Homeowners should approach cash-out refinancing carefully and strategically. Using home equity for temporary consumption, vacations, luxury purchases, or depreciating assets often weakens long-term financial positioning. Using equity to improve long-term cash flow or reduce higher-interest obligations may sometimes create financial benefits if executed responsibly.

Timing also matters greatly in refinancing decisions. Interest rate environments shift over time based on economic conditions, inflation, monetary policy, and financial markets. Homeowners who understand rate cycles and remain financially prepared may take advantage of favorable opportunities when rates decline. However, attempting to perfectly predict interest rate movements is extremely difficult. Refinancing decisions should focus more on whether the new structure improves long-term financial positioning rather than attempting to time markets perfectly.

Another critical factor in refinancing is closing costs. Refinancing is not free. Costs may include lender fees, appraisal fees, title expenses, recording fees, and other charges. Homeowners must calculate whether projected savings outweigh these upfront costs over a reasonable timeframe.

One useful calculation is the break-even point. This measures how long it takes for monthly savings to recover refinancing costs. For example, if refinancing costs $5,000 and monthly savings equal $250, the break-even period is approximately twenty months. If the homeowner plans to stay in the property much longer, refinancing may make strong financial sense.

Still, monthly savings alone should not be the only consideration. Some refinances slightly increase monthly payments while dramatically reducing total interest and shortening payoff timelines. Long-term wealth preservation often matters more than short-term payment reduction.

Homeowners should also avoid excessive refinancing frequency. Constant refinancing may create fee accumulation, extended debt timelines, and financial confusion. Strategic refinancing should support clear long-term goals rather than reacting emotionally to every market fluctuation.

One of the most important questions homeowners should ask before refinancing is: "What is the purpose of this refinance?" Without a clear purpose, refinancing can become financially dangerous. The goal may be lowering interest, accelerating payoff, improving cash flow, removing mortgage insurance, consolidating debt, or strengthening long-term stability. Clarity matters.

Refinancing also interacts heavily with personal psychology. Many homeowners feel emotionally attached to lower monthly payments because lower obligations feel safer. Others become overly aggressive and choose extremely high payments that strain daily life unnecessarily. The ideal strategy balances acceleration with sustainability.

Another common refinancing mistake involves focusing only on payment reduction while increasing total debt dramatically through repeated cash-out borrowing. Some homeowners continually extract equity to finance lifestyle spending, leaving themselves highly leveraged even after many years of ownership. This behavior often delays wealth creation significantly. True mortgage acceleration requires intentionality. Refinancing should strengthen financial positioning rather than simply creating temporary emotional relief or funding unsustainable lifestyles.

Another powerful strategy homeowners use involves refinancing while continuing previous payment levels. For example, if refinancing reduces a mortgage payment from $3,000 to $2,400 monthly, the homeowner may continue voluntarily paying $3,000. The extra $600 accelerates principal reduction substantially because the lower interest structure increases efficiency.

This strategy can dramatically shorten loan terms while maintaining financial flexibility. If hardship occurs, the homeowner still has the lower required payment available temporarily.

Refinancing may also become particularly valuable during periods of rising homeowner income. A homeowner whose earnings have increased substantially since the original purchase may refinance into shorter terms more comfortably than earlier in life. Career growth often creates opportunities for more aggressive acceleration strategies later.

Another important benefit of refinancing strategically is improved long-term cash flow management. Lower rates reduce interest waste. Reduced interest waste increases available future capital. That capital may later support investing, retirement planning, business growth, travel, family goals, or earlier financial independence.

Mortgage interest represents one of the largest long-term expenses most families ever pay. Even moderate reductions in total interest can dramatically reshape long-term financial outcomes.

Importantly, homeowners should avoid emotional decision-making during refinancing. Mortgage advertisements often focus heavily on payment reductions without emphasizing total interest costs, extended timelines, or long-term implications. Financial decisions should be based on complete analysis rather than marketing excitement.

Working with knowledgeable mortgage professionals can help homeowners evaluate refinancing scenarios carefully. Homeowners should compare multiple loan structures, rates, fees, timelines, and payoff projections before making decisions. Small structural differences may create enormous long-term outcomes.

Refinancing also creates opportunities for strategic resets. Some homeowners refinance after eliminating consumer debt, increasing income, improving credit scores, or strengthening financial stability. Better financial positioning often leads to better loan terms and lower long-term borrowing costs.

Credit improvement alone can significantly influence refinancing outcomes. Higher credit scores often qualify borrowers for lower rates, improved pricing, and better loan structures. This highlights the importance of broader financial health alongside mortgage management.

One of the greatest emotional benefits of strategic refinancing is regaining control. Many homeowners initially feel trapped by unfavorable loan terms or rising obligations. A well-executed refinance can improve confidence, reduce stress, and create a clearer path toward financial freedom.

However, homeowners must remember that refinancing is not magic. It does not automatically solve financial problems caused by overspending, poor cash flow management, or uncontrolled debt accumulation. Refinancing works best when combined with disciplined financial behavior and intentional planning.

Ultimately, refinancing is most powerful when viewed as part of a larger wealth acceleration strategy rather than an isolated transaction. The objective is not merely obtaining a new loan. The objective is improving long-term financial positioning.

The homeowner who understands refinancing strategically begins seeing mortgages differently. Instead of passively accepting loan terms forever, they recognize opportunities to optimize, restructure, and accelerate progress intentionally.

That awareness transforms the mortgage from a fixed burden into a flexible financial tool.

How Strategic Refinancing Can Save Hundreds of Thousands of Dollars

Let's examine a realistic refinancing scenario to understand how refinancing strategically can dramatically reduce long-term interest costs and accelerate mortgage payoff.

Original Mortgage Scenario

- Original Loan Amount: $450,000
- Original Interest Rate: 7.25% fixed
- Original Loan Term: 30 years
- Original Monthly Principal & Interest Payment: Approximately $3,070
- Total Interest Over 30 Years: Approximately $655,000

After five years of payments, the homeowner still owes approximately:

- Remaining Mortgage Balance: Approximately $423,000

Now imagine market interest rates decline, and the homeowner qualifies for refinancing.

Refinancing Scenario

New Loan Terms

- New Loan Amount: $423,000
- New Interest Rate: 5.25% fixed
- New Loan Term: 20 years
- New Monthly Principal & Interest Payment: Approximately $2,850

Immediate Benefits

- Monthly Payment Reduced Slightly
- Loan Term Reduced by 5 Years
- Interest Rate Reduced by 2%

Long-Term Results

Original Remaining Scenario Without Refinancing

If the homeowner kept the original loan:

- Remaining Payments: Approximately 25 years
- Remaining Interest to Be Paid: Approximately $498,000

After Refinancing

With the new refinance:

- Remaining Interest to Be Paid: Approximately $261,000

Estimated Interest Savings

- Approximately $237,000 saved in future interest

Additional Benefit

- Mortgage paid off approximately 5 years earlier

This means the homeowner:

- Lowers the payment slightly
- Pays off the mortgage faster

- Saves nearly a quarter million dollars in interest

Hybrid Strategy Example

Now let's examine an even more powerful strategy.

Suppose the homeowner refinances into a new 30-year loan at 5.25% to maximize flexibility.

New 30-Year Loan Payment

- Approximately $2,335 monthly

Instead of reducing spending, the homeowner continues paying the old payment amount of $3,070 voluntarily.

Extra Principal Applied Monthly

- Extra Principal: Approximately $735 monthly

Results

- Mortgage Paid Off in Approximately 17 Years Instead of 30
- Estimated Interest Savings: Approximately $295,000

This strategy creates:

- Lower required payment flexibility during emergencies

- Faster payoff when financially comfortable
- Massive long-term interest savings

Important Lesson

Refinancing is not just about lowering monthly payments.

When used strategically, refinancing can:

- Lower interest costs dramatically
- Accelerate mortgage payoff
- Improve monthly cash flow
- Increase financial flexibility
- Reduce long-term debt exposure
- Save hundreds of thousands of dollars

The key is understanding the entire financial picture rather than focusing only on the monthly payment amount.

Smart refinancing is not about restarting debt blindly.

It is about restructuring debt intelligently.

Chapter 8

Using Extra Income Streams to Accelerate Mortgage Freedom Without Financial Stress

One of the most powerful ways to accelerate mortgage payoff without sacrificing lifestyle quality is by increasing income intentionally rather than relying exclusively on expense reduction. While budgeting and cash flow optimization are essential, there is a practical limit to how much most households can cut expenses. Income, however, often has far greater growth potential. Even relatively modest additional income streams can dramatically accelerate mortgage payoff timelines when used strategically and consistently.

Many homeowners initially believe they must choose between enjoying life and paying off their mortgage faster. In reality, additional income can create a bridge between those goals. Instead of reducing every enjoyable expense, homeowners can generate extra cash flow specifically dedicated to principal reduction. This approach often feels more empowering psychologically because the homeowner is expanding opportunity rather than simply restricting spending. An income acceleration strategy does not necessarily require quitting a full-time job, starting a massive company, or working eighty-hour weeks. Some of the most effective extra income streams begin small and grow gradually over time. Freelancing, consulting, tutoring, coaching, online businesses, digital products, rental income, weekend work, content creation, seasonal work, or monetizing existing skills can all contribute meaningful amounts toward mortgage reduction.

The key concept is intentional allocation. Extra income only accelerates financial freedom when it is directed strategically rather than absorbed automatically into lifestyle inflation. Many people earn more money over time but never feel financially stronger because additional income disappears into upgraded spending habits. Without intentional systems, higher income alone does not guarantee progress.

This is why many financially disciplined homeowners create specific rules for handling extra income. For example, they may decide that all side-business income goes toward mortgage principal. Others split additional earnings among savings, investing, enjoyment, and debt reduction. Creating predefined allocation systems removes emotional decision-making and improves consistency.

One important psychological advantage of using extra income for mortgage acceleration is that it often feels less painful than reducing normal spending. A homeowner may feel emotionally attached to existing lifestyle habits, but additional income streams create new financial capacity without necessarily requiring major sacrifices. This makes the strategy easier to sustain long term.

Another powerful aspect of extra income is flexibility. Homeowners can scale additional work or projects up or down depending on life circumstances, energy levels, family needs, and financial goals. During periods of strong motivation or favorable opportunities, income acceleration may increase significantly. During stressful periods, homeowners can temporarily reduce extra efforts without completely abandoning the overall mortgage strategy.

One of the most common and accessible forms of extra income is freelancing or consulting based on existing professional skills. Many individuals possess expertise that others are willing to pay for outside normal employment hours. Accountants, teachers, designers, writers, programmers, marketers, contractors, photographers, mortgage professionals, fitness coaches, and countless other professionals often have monetizable knowledge.

The advantage of skill-based side income is that startup costs are often relatively low because the homeowner already possesses the expertise. Even a few hundred dollars monthly directed consistently toward mortgage principal can create substantial long-term savings.

Digital income opportunities have also expanded dramatically in recent years. Many homeowners now generate income through online courses, ebooks, affiliate marketing, social media content, YouTube channels, coaching programs, templates, newsletters, AI-assisted services, or ecommerce businesses. While not every project becomes highly profitable immediately, even moderate online income streams can accelerate mortgage reduction meaningfully.

Rental income is another powerful mortgage acceleration tool. Some homeowners rent spare rooms, accessory dwelling units, vacation properties, or portions of their homes strategically. Others use house hacking strategies, where tenants help offset mortgage costs significantly. Rental cash flow can dramatically reduce the homeowner's personal housing burden while increasing long-term wealth simultaneously.

Importantly, homeowners should not underestimate the power of modest consistent income. Many people dismiss side opportunities because the income initially seems "too small to matter." But mortgage acceleration compounds over time. An extra five hundred dollars monthly applied toward principal over many years can remove substantial time from a mortgage while saving enormous amounts in future interest.

Time magnifies disciplined action. Small extra income streams that continue consistently often produce surprisingly large long-term outcomes.

Another major advantage of extra income strategies is emotional empowerment. Many homeowners feel trapped because they view their income as fixed and unchangeable. Developing additional income streams shifts mindset dramatically. Instead of feeling limited by one paycheck, the homeowner begins recognizing opportunities for growth and financial control.

This mindset shift can become transformational beyond the mortgage itself. Individuals who successfully generate side income often build confidence, entrepreneurial thinking, financial creativity, and long-term wealth-building habits. Mortgage acceleration becomes the starting point for broader financial expansion.

However, homeowners should also avoid burnout. One common mistake is becoming overly aggressive with side work to the point that physical health, relationships, sleep, or emotional well-being deteriorate. Financial freedom should improve quality of life rather than destroy it. Sustainable income strategies are usually more effective long term than exhausting short-term intensity.

Balance remains essential. Some seasons of life may support aggressive side income generation more comfortably than others. Families with young children, demanding careers, health challenges, or caregiving responsibilities may require more moderate approaches. The ideal strategy is not the most extreme strategy. It is the strategy that can be sustained consistently while preserving overall well-being.

Another important principle is separating productive income from consumptive income mentally. Many financially successful homeowners create dedicated accounts for side-business income or bonus earnings. This separation reduces the temptation to spend additional income impulsively and reinforces intentional financial behavior.

For example, a homeowner might create a "Mortgage Freedom Account" specifically for all side income deposits. Every dollar entering the account becomes psychologically connected to long-term freedom rather than short-term consumption. This simple behavioral system can significantly improve consistency.

Tax planning also becomes increasingly important as additional income grows. Side income may create self-employment tax obligations, estimated taxes, or deductible business expenses. Homeowners should educate themselves appropriately or work with qualified tax professionals to maximize efficiency and compliance.

One powerful long-term strategy involves redirecting income from eliminated debts toward the mortgage. For example, once a vehicle loan or student loan is paid off, the former monthly payment can immediately begin accelerating mortgage principal. This creates increasing momentum over time without requiring lifestyle reduction.

Momentum is one of the most important concepts in financial acceleration. As debts disappear and income increases, more cash flow becomes available for wealth-building. Mortgage reduction speeds up gradually, then more dramatically later. What initially feels slow eventually becomes powerful.

Another overlooked source of extra income is skill monetization within existing careers. Many employees fail to negotiate raises, pursue certifications, seek promotions, or leverage expertise effectively. Career optimization itself can become a mortgage acceleration strategy. Even moderate salary increases applied strategically can dramatically improve long-term outcomes.

For example, if a homeowner receives a $1,000 monthly after-tax raise and directs even half toward principal reduction consistently, the long-term mortgage impact can become enormous. The combination of rising income and disciplined allocation creates accelerating results.

Homeowners should also understand the emotional difference between active income and passive income. Active income requires direct time and effort continuously, while passive income may continue producing revenue after initial setup. Examples of passive or semi-passive income may include rental properties, digital products, royalties, dividends, online courses, or automated businesses.

While building passive income often requires significant initial effort, successful passive income streams can dramatically accelerate mortgage freedom over time. Many financially independent individuals eventually focus heavily on increasing passive cash flow because it reduces dependency on active labor income.

Still, homeowners should remain realistic. Not every side hustle becomes highly profitable immediately. Some projects fail. Some income streams fluctuate unpredictably. Some opportunities require time before generating meaningful revenue. Patience and experimentation matter.

The purpose is not perfection. The purpose is increasing financial flexibility gradually over time.

Another important issue homeowners must avoid is allowing extra income to justify excessive new spending. This is a subtle but common trap. As income rises, individuals often unconsciously upgrade lifestyles immediately, leaving little actual improvement in long-term financial freedom.

This phenomenon explains why some very high-income households remain financially stressed despite impressive earnings. Without intentional allocation systems, lifestyle inflation consumes progress rapidly.

Financially disciplined homeowners often choose controlled lifestyle growth instead. They improve quality of life thoughtfully while still directing meaningful portions of increased income toward debt reduction, investing, and long-term stability.

One useful strategy is percentage allocation. For example:

- 50% of extra income toward mortgage payoff
- 25% toward investing or savings
- 25% toward enjoyment or lifestyle improvement

This balanced approach creates both present enjoyment and future acceleration simultaneously. Extra income also improves financial resilience. Homeowners with multiple income sources often experience greater stability during economic uncertainty, layoffs, or industry changes. Diversified income streams reduce dependency on a single paycheck and strengthen overall financial positioning.

This resilience becomes especially valuable during difficult economic periods. A homeowner with side income, savings, and reduced debt obligations typically experiences far less financial anxiety than someone fully dependent on one income source with high obligations.

Another psychological benefit of using extra income strategically is increased confidence. Each extra principal payment funded by additional income represents visible proof that the homeowner is taking control of their future actively. Confidence builds through action.

The mortgage gradually transforms from something that feels permanent into something increasingly manageable and temporary. This emotional shift changes behavior throughout the entire financial life of the homeowner.

Importantly, homeowners should celebrate progress along the way. Every milestone matters. Eliminating one year from the mortgage schedule matters. Reaching a major principal reduction target matters. Building the first successful side income stream matters. Recognizing progress reinforces momentum and motivation.

The combination of extra income and strategic mortgage acceleration can become extraordinarily powerful because it attacks debt from both directions simultaneously: improving cash flow while reducing long-term interest exposure.

Ultimately, the purpose of extra income is not merely working more. The deeper purpose is buying back freedom faster. Every dollar directed strategically toward mortgage principal today may eliminate multiple future dollars of obligations and interest.

That trade-off becomes incredibly valuable over time.

The homeowner who understands this no longer sees extra income as temporary spending money alone.

They begin seeing it as a tool capable of permanently reshaping their future.

How an Extra Income Stream Can Remove More Than a Decade from a Mortgage

Let's examine a realistic scenario to understand how powerful extra income can become when applied consistently toward mortgage acceleration.

Original Mortgage Scenario

- Loan Amount: $425,000
- Interest Rate: 6.75% fixed
- Loan Term: 30 years
- Monthly Principal & Interest Payment: Approximately $2,757
- Total Interest Over 30 Years: Approximately $567,500

Most homeowners focus only on the monthly payment. However, over thirty years, the homeowner pays more than half a million dollars in interest.

Now let's see what happens when the homeowner creates an additional income stream.

Extra Income Scenario

The homeowner starts a side business generating:

- $1,000 per month in additional after-tax income

Instead of spending this money, they apply the entire amount directly toward mortgage principal every month.

New Total Monthly Payment

- Original Mortgage Payment: $2,757
- Extra Principal Payment: $1,000
- Total Monthly Payment: $3,757

Results

Mortgage Payoff Timeline

- Original Mortgage Term: 30 years
- New Estimated Payoff Time: Approximately 16 years and 8 months

Time Saved

- More Than 13 Years Removed from the Mortgage

Estimated Interest Savings

- Approximately $301,000 Saved in Interest

This means a relatively moderate side income stream can:

- Cut the mortgage timeline nearly in half
- Save over three hundred thousand dollars
- Create mortgage freedom more than a decade earlier

Even Smaller Income Example

Now let's examine a smaller extra income stream.

Additional Side Income

- $400 monthly from tutoring, freelancing, consulting, or online sales

Results

- Mortgage Payoff Time Reduced to Approximately 22 Years
- Time Saved: About 8 Years
- Estimated Interest Saved: Approximately $175,000

Even modest consistent extra income creates enormous long-term financial impact.

Hybrid Strategy Example

Now let's combine multiple smaller strategies.

Combined Strategy

- $500 monthly side income applied to principal
- One extra annual mortgage payment
- Annual tax refund lump sum of $3,000 applied to principal

Results

- Mortgage Payoff Time Reduced From 30 Years to Approximately 15 Years and 9 Months
- Total Time Saved: More Than 14 Years
- Estimated Interest Saved: Approximately $338,000

This demonstrates how combining several moderate strategies can create extraordinary acceleration.

Key Lesson

Extra income becomes transformational when paired with intentional allocation.

A side income stream is not just extra spending money.

When applied strategically, it can:

- Remove years from your mortgage

- Save hundreds of thousands in interest
- Increase equity dramatically faster
- Reduce financial stress
- Accelerate long-term financial freedom

Small consistent income streams often create life-changing outcomes over time when directed intentionally instead of emotionally.

Chapter 9

Balancing Mortgage Payoff with Investing to Build Long-Term Wealth Faster

One of the most important and controversial financial questions homeowners eventually face is whether extra money should be directed toward paying off the mortgage faster or invested for long-term growth. Some people believe eliminating mortgage debt as quickly as possible is always the smartest financial decision. Others argue that investing excess money can potentially produce higher long-term returns than accelerated mortgage reduction. The truth is more nuanced. The best strategy depends on mathematics, psychology, risk tolerance, cash flow stability, interest rates, and personal financial goals.

Understanding how to balance mortgage payoff and investing strategically is essential because both decisions influence long-term wealth creation dramatically. A mortgage is not just a monthly payment. It is also a financial obligation with an interest cost. Investments, meanwhile, represent assets that may potentially grow and compound over time. The challenge is deciding how to allocate limited financial resources between reducing debt and building future wealth simultaneously.

Many homeowners approach this topic emotionally rather than strategically. Some become obsessed with debt elimination because carrying any mortgage balance creates stress or anxiety. Others avoid mortgage acceleration completely because they assume investing always produces better returns. Neither extreme is automatically correct. Intelligent financial planning usually involves evaluating both sides carefully and creating a balanced strategy aligned with long-term objectives.

The first important concept homeowners must understand is guaranteed return versus potential return. Every extra principal payment toward a mortgage produces a guaranteed return equal to the mortgage interest rate. For example, paying down a mortgage carrying 7% interest effectively creates a guaranteed 7% savings because the homeowner avoids future interest costs on that money.

Investments, on the other hand, may potentially earn higher returns over long periods, but investment returns are not guaranteed. Markets fluctuate. Economic conditions change. Investments carry varying levels of risk. This distinction matters because risk tolerance differs greatly between individuals. For some homeowners, the guaranteed return of mortgage payoff combined with reduced financial stress creates enormous value emotionally and financially. Others are comfortable accepting market volatility in pursuit of potentially higher long-term investment growth. The right answer often depends as much on personal psychology as mathematics.

Another major factor is mortgage interest rates. The higher the mortgage rate, the more attractive accelerated payoff becomes financially. For example, a homeowner carrying a 7.5% mortgage may benefit substantially from aggressive payoff because eliminating that interest expense creates strong guaranteed savings. Conversely, someone with a very low fixed mortgage rate may prioritize investing more heavily while maintaining manageable debt.

Time horizon also matters greatly. Younger homeowners with decades until retirement may benefit from balancing investing aggressively alongside mortgage reduction because long-term investment compounding can become extremely powerful over time. Older homeowners approaching retirement may prioritize debt elimination more heavily to reduce future financial obligations and increase stability.

One important principle many financially successful individuals follow is diversification of financial progress.

Instead of choosing only one path, they combine mortgage acceleration with investing simultaneously. This balanced approach reduces debt gradually while also building investment assets over time. The homeowner gains both increasing equity and growing investment accounts rather than relying entirely on one strategy.

This balanced approach often creates psychological advantages as well. Homeowners avoid feeling overly restricted because they are improving multiple areas of financial health simultaneously. They build security through debt reduction while also creating future wealth opportunities through investing.

Retirement investing deserves special attention in this discussion. Many homeowners become so focused on paying off the mortgage that they neglect retirement contributions entirely. This can become financially dangerous because retirement accounts benefit enormously from long-term compounding and tax advantages. Missing years of retirement investing may create larger long-term consequences than carrying a moderate mortgage balance slightly longer.

For example, employer-sponsored retirement plans with matching contributions often provide immediate returns that exceed mortgage interest savings. A homeowner who ignores retirement matching opportunities to accelerate mortgage payoff may unintentionally lose substantial long-term wealth-building advantages.

This is why balance matters so much. Mortgage reduction should strengthen long-term financial freedom, not weaken overall financial positioning. Homeowners should evaluate retirement planning, emergency savings, insurance protection, and investment opportunities alongside debt reduction goals.

Another major factor is liquidity. Money applied toward mortgage principal becomes tied up in home equity. While home equity increases net worth, it is less liquid than cash or investment accounts. Accessing home equity later often requires borrowing again through refinancing, home equity loans, or selling the property.

Investments and savings accounts may provide greater flexibility during emergencies or opportunities. Homeowners who aggressively eliminate mortgage debt without maintaining sufficient liquid assets may feel financially constrained despite strong equity positions.

This does not mean mortgage payoff is unwise. It simply highlights the importance of balance and strategic planning. Financial freedom involves both reducing obligations and maintaining flexibility. Inflation also plays a role in this discussion. Fixed-rate mortgages become less expensive in real terms over time because inflation gradually reduces the future purchasing power of money. If incomes rise over time while the mortgage payment remains fixed, the payment may feel relatively smaller years later.

Some investors therefore prefer maintaining low fixed-rate debt while directing excess cash toward appreciating investments. Others still prioritize debt elimination because they value certainty, simplicity, and reduced obligations more than maximizing theoretical investment returns.

Behavioral finance is another important consideration. Financial success depends not only on theoretical optimization but also on actual behavior. Some homeowners simply sleep better knowing their debt is disappearing quickly. Others feel more motivated watching investment accounts grow. The most mathematically optimal plan is meaningless if it creates emotional stress severe enough to cause inconsistent behavior or poor decision-making.

One powerful strategy homeowners use is establishing percentage-based allocation systems. For example:

- 50% of extra cash flow toward mortgage principal
- 30% toward investing

- 20% toward savings or lifestyle goals

This balanced structure allows progress across multiple financial areas simultaneously while avoiding extreme positions.

Another effective strategy involves milestone-based planning. Some homeowners focus aggressively on mortgage reduction until reaching certain equity or balance targets, then shift more heavily toward investing afterward. Others prioritize retirement account contributions first, then direct additional cash flow toward the mortgage after investment goals are satisfied.

The ideal structure depends on personal priorities and financial circumstances.

One critical mistake homeowners should avoid is assuming investment returns are automatic or guaranteed. Historical stock market returns may average strong long-term growth, but markets experience volatility, recessions, and downturns. Homeowners using leverage and investing simultaneously must remain emotionally prepared for periods where investments decline while mortgage obligations remain fixed.

Risk tolerance therefore matters enormously. Some individuals remain comfortable during market volatility, while others experience severe stress. A strategy only works if the homeowner can maintain discipline during difficult periods. Another important issue is tax efficiency. Mortgage interest may provide tax benefits for some homeowners depending on income, deductions, and tax law changes. Investment accounts may also create tax advantages depending on structure. Homeowners should evaluate these factors carefully, particularly when making large financial allocation decisions.

As homeowners progress financially, many eventually recognize that wealth-building is not simply about maximizing net worth mathematically. It is also about creating freedom, flexibility, peace of mind, and life options. For some individuals, becoming completely debt-free produces emotional freedom worth more than maximizing every possible investment dollar.

Others feel comfortable carrying manageable mortgage debt while aggressively building businesses, investments, or income-producing assets. Again, neither approach is universally correct.

One of the most effective long-term strategies often involves gradual transition. Early in life, homeowners may prioritize investing heavily while making moderate mortgage acceleration payments. Later, as income increases and investments grow, they may accelerate mortgage reduction more aggressively approaching retirement. This strategy allows investment compounding to work for decades while still reducing long-term obligations before retirement years. Flexibility and adaptability are key.

Another important concept is cash flow leverage. A paid-off mortgage dramatically increases monthly free cash flow. Once the mortgage disappears, thousands of dollars monthly may become available for investing, travel, family support, entrepreneurship, or retirement lifestyle improvements.

This future cash flow increase can itself become a wealth-building engine. Homeowners who eliminate mortgages earlier often later redirect former mortgage payments into investment accounts aggressively.

For example, a homeowner paying $3,000 monthly toward a mortgage who later redirects that same amount into investments may create substantial long-term wealth acceleration. Mortgage payoff and investing therefore do not necessarily compete permanently. Often, they occur sequentially over time.

Another powerful benefit of mortgage reduction is reduced required income levels. Homeowners with lower monthly obligations need less income to maintain stability. This creates career flexibility, entrepreneurial opportunities, earlier retirement potential, and reduced financial pressure. Many people underestimate how much emotional freedom lower obligations create. A person requiring $12,000 monthly to maintain lifestyle experiences very different stress levels than someone requiring $5,000 monthly. Mortgage reduction can dramatically lower required living expenses long term.

Homeowners should also remember that markets, interest rates, inflation, and economic conditions change over time. Financial strategies should remain flexible rather than rigid. Periodic review helps ensure the plan continues aligning with goals and circumstances.

One important lesson many financially successful individuals eventually learn is that wealth-building rarely depends on one perfect strategy alone. Long-term financial success usually results from consistent disciplined behavior across multiple areas simultaneously: earning, saving, investing, reducing debt, managing risk, and controlling lifestyle inflation.

Mortgage acceleration becomes most powerful when integrated into a broader financial framework rather than treated as an isolated goal.

Another important mindset shift involves recognizing that financial freedom is deeply personal. Some homeowners prioritize peace and simplicity. Others prioritize maximum asset growth. Some value security above all else. Others embrace calculated financial leverage comfortably. There is no universally correct emotional relationship with debt. The key is ensuring decisions are intentional, informed, and aligned with long-term values rather than driven purely by fear, ego, or social pressure.

Ultimately, balancing mortgage payoff and investing is not about choosing one side permanently. It is about understanding trade-offs and building a strategy that creates both present stability and future opportunity.

The homeowner who learns to balance debt reduction with wealth creation intelligently gains enormous long-term advantage. They avoid becoming overly leveraged while also avoiding missed opportunities for long-term growth.

Most importantly, they stop viewing financial decisions in extremes and begin thinking strategically.

That strategic thinking changes everything.

Comparing Mortgage Payoff vs Investing Over 30 Years

Let's examine a realistic scenario to understand how balancing mortgage payoff and investing can impact long-term wealth.

Original Mortgage Scenario

- Mortgage Balance: $400,000
- Interest Rate: 6.75% fixed
- Loan Term: 30 years
- Monthly Principal & Interest Payment: Approximately $2,594
- Total Interest Over 30 Years: Approximately $533,800

Now let's assume the homeowner has an extra:

- $1,000 per month available for financial goals

The homeowner now faces two possible strategies.

Strategy 1: Aggressive Mortgage Payoff

The homeowner applies the full extra $1,000 monthly toward mortgage principal.

Results

Total Monthly Payment

- Original Payment: $2,594
- Extra Principal: $1,000

- Total Payment: $3,594

Mortgage Payoff Timeline

- Mortgage Paid Off in Approximately 15 Years and 2 Months

Interest Savings

- Estimated Interest Saved: Approximately $287,000

Major Benefit

After year 15, the homeowner now has:

- No mortgage payment
- An additional $3,594 monthly cash flow available

If the homeowner then invests that $3,594 monthly for the remaining 15 years at a hypothetical 8% annual return:

Estimated Investment Value After 15 Years

- Approximately $1.25 million

Strategy 2: Invest the Extra $1,000 Instead

Now let's assume the homeowner makes only the required mortgage payment and invests the extra $1,000 monthly immediately instead.

Mortgage Timeline

- Full 30-year mortgage remains in place

Total Interest Paid

- Approximately $533,800

Investment Growth

If the homeowner invests:

- $1,000 monthly
- At a hypothetical 8% annual return
- For the full 30 years

Estimated Investment Value After 30 Years

- Approximately $1.49 million

Comparing the Outcomes

Strategy 1: Mortgage First

Benefits

- Mortgage eliminated in 15 years
- Interest savings of approximately $287,000

- Increased cash flow earlier
- Lower financial stress
- Greater flexibility sooner

Estimated Investment Value by Year 30

- Approximately $1.25 million after investing former mortgage payments for 15 years

Strategy 2: Invest First

Benefits

- Larger long-term investment account
- More liquidity throughout the process
- Potentially greater total wealth mathematically

Estimated Investment Value by Year 30

- Approximately $1.49 million

Trade-Off

- Mortgage remains for full 30 years
- Higher long-term interest paid

- Higher required monthly obligations longer

Balanced Hybrid Strategy Example

Now let's examine a balanced approach.

Hybrid Allocation

- $500 monthly toward mortgage principal
- $500 monthly toward investing

Mortgage Results

- Mortgage Paid Off in Approximately 20 Years
- Interest Saved: Approximately $177,000

Investment Results

- $500 invested monthly for 30 years at hypothetical 8% return
- Estimated Investment Value: Approximately $745,000

Additional Opportunity

After mortgage payoff in year 20:

- Former mortgage payment can now also be invested for remaining years

This creates:

- Strong investment growth
- Reduced long-term debt
- Balanced flexibility and security

Key Lesson

There is no single perfect answer for every homeowner.

The best strategy depends on:

- Interest rates
- Risk tolerance
- Emotional comfort with debt
- Retirement goals
- Cash flow stability
- Investment discipline
- Lifestyle priorities

The important thing is making intentional decisions rather than operating on autopilot.

Mortgage payoff and investing do not need to compete against each other.

When balanced strategically, they can work together to create long-term financial freedom.

Chapter 10

The Ultimate Mortgage Payoff Game Plan: Combining Every Strategy Into a Clear Path to Financial Freedom

Reaching mortgage freedom is rarely the result of a single strategy. Instead, it is usually the outcome of combining multiple approaches consistently over time in a structured and intentional way. Throughout this series, we have explored biweekly payments, lump sum contributions, refinancing, cash flow optimization, income generation, investing balance strategies, and mindset development. The final step is learning how to combine all of these methods into a unified mortgage payoff game plan that fits real life, not just theory.

Many homeowners fail to reach their financial goals because they treat mortgage payoff strategies as isolated techniques rather than a connected system. They may try extra payments for a few months, then stop. They may refinance once, but never optimize again. They may generate extra income but fail to allocate it consistently. Without a cohesive system, progress becomes inconsistent and motivation fades.

The ultimate mortgage payoff game plan is designed to solve that problem by creating structure, clarity, and long-term consistency. It is not about doing everything perfectly. It is about building a repeatable financial system that works over many years regardless of income fluctuations, life changes, or economic conditions.

The first principle of the ultimate game plan is cash flow awareness. Every mortgage payoff strategy depends on understanding how money moves in and out of your household. Without clear awareness of income, expenses, and available surplus, it becomes impossible to consistently direct money toward principal reduction or investing.

Cash flow awareness begins with tracking. Homeowners must understand their fixed expenses, variable spending, and discretionary habits. This does not require extreme budgeting or restrictive behavior. Instead, it requires clarity. Once clarity exists, decisions become intentional rather than automatic.

The second principle is structured allocation. Instead of randomly deciding where extra money goes each month, homeowners should create a defined system. For example, extra cash flow may be divided into three categories: mortgage principal reduction, investing or savings, and lifestyle enjoyment. This prevents financial imbalance and reduces emotional decision fatigue. Structured allocation ensures that progress happens in multiple areas simultaneously. Mortgage debt decreases, wealth-building increases, and quality of life remains intact. This balance is what makes long-term financial success sustainable.

The third principle is automation. Automation transforms financial behavior from effort-based to system-based. When payments, transfers, and allocations happen automatically, consistency increases dramatically. Many homeowners fail not because they lack knowledge, but because they rely too heavily on motivation. Automation removes this weakness.

Automating extra mortgage payments, investment contributions, or savings transfers ensures progress continues even during busy or stressful periods. Over time, automation becomes one of the most powerful tools in financial acceleration because it eliminates inconsistency.

The fourth principle is income expansion. While reducing expenses and optimizing cash flow are important, increasing income often creates the greatest acceleration potential. Side income, bonuses, commissions, freelance work, consulting, or business ventures can significantly shorten mortgage timelines when directed intentionally.

However, income expansion only works when paired with disciplined allocation. Without structure, increased income simply leads to lifestyle inflation. With structure, it becomes a powerful wealth-building engine.

The fifth principle is strategic lump sum deployment. Windfalls such as tax refunds, bonuses, inheritances, or investment gains should not be treated as automatic spending opportunities. Instead, they should be evaluated strategically and allocated intentionally.

Even partial allocation of lump sums toward mortgage reduction can dramatically shorten loan timelines. Over many years, these irregular but powerful contributions can remove large portions of mortgage debt and save substantial interest.

The sixth principle is interest awareness. Every mortgage decision ultimately affects total interest paid over time. Whether through refinancing, extra payments, or timing strategies, reducing interest is one of the most powerful financial levers available to homeowners.

Understanding interest transforms behavior. Homeowners begin to see every extra dollar applied toward principal as a reduction in future financial burden. This awareness alone often leads to better financial decisions.

The seventh principle is flexibility. Life is unpredictable. Income changes, expenses rise, emergencies occur, and financial priorities shift over time. A rigid mortgage payoff plan often fails because it cannot adapt to reality.

A flexible game plan allows homeowners to increase or decrease acceleration strategies depending on circumstances without abandoning long-term goals. Flexibility ensures sustainability, which is more important than intensity.

The eighth principle is psychological alignment. Mortgage payoff strategies must align with emotional comfort, lifestyle preferences, and long-term values. A strategy that creates constant stress is unlikely to last. A strategy that balances discipline with enjoyment is far more sustainable.

Financial success is not just about numbers. It is about behavior. And behavior is driven by psychology. Homeowners must feel ownership over their plan rather than pressure from it.

The ninth principle is progress tracking. What gets measured improves. Many homeowners lose motivation because progress feels invisible. Tracking mortgage balance reduction, interest savings, equity growth, and timeline changes transforms abstract effort into visible results.

When progress becomes visible, motivation increases. When motivation increases, consistency improves. When consistency improves, financial outcomes accelerate. The tenth and final principle is long-term integration. Mortgage payoff should not exist in isolation. It should integrate with investing, retirement planning, emergency savings, and overall wealth strategy. The ultimate goal is not just owning a home outright, but building complete financial independence.

A fully integrated plan ensures that eliminating a mortgage becomes one part of a larger wealth-building system rather than the only focus.

When all ten principles are combined, homeowners create a powerful financial ecosystem. Income flows in, expenses are controlled, extra cash is allocated intentionally, windfalls are used strategically, interest is minimized, and progress is tracked consistently. Over time, this system compounds into significant financial transformation.

The ultimate mortgage payoff game plan is not about perfection. It is about alignment, structure, and consistency. Even modest actions become powerful when applied repeatedly within a strong system. Small monthly improvements, occasional lump sums, strategic refinancing, and additional income all work together to shorten timelines and reduce long-term interest dramatically.

Homeowners who adopt this system begin to experience a shift in identity. They stop seeing themselves as passive borrowers and begin seeing themselves as active wealth builders. The mortgage becomes something they are managing intentionally rather than something they are simply enduring.

This shift is the true purpose of the entire series. Mortgage freedom is not just about eliminating debt. It is about gaining control over financial life, increasing options, reducing stress, and building long-term independence.

When homeowners reach the point where their system runs consistently and their financial behavior becomes second nature, mortgage payoff is no longer uncertain. It becomes inevitable.

The ultimate game plan works because it combines knowledge, behavior, structure, and time into a single unified approach.

And over time, that combination changes everything.

The Complete Mortgage Payoff System in Action

Let's bring everything together into a realistic example showing how multiple strategies combine to dramatically accelerate mortgage freedom.

Original Mortgage Scenario

- Loan Amount: $375,000

- Interest Rate: 6.50% fixed
- Loan Term: 30 years
- Monthly Principal & Interest Payment: Approximately $2,370
- Total Interest Over 30 Years: Approximately $478,000

Now let's apply the full mortgage payoff game plan step by step.

Step 1: Biweekly Payment Strategy

Instead of monthly payments:

- Half payment every 2 weeks = $1,185
- Equivalent of 13 payments per year instead of 12

Result:

- Mortgage shortened by approximately 5 years
- Interest saved: approximately $95,000

Step 2: Extra Monthly Cash Flow Allocation

Homeowner applies:

- $400 monthly extra principal payment

Result:

- Additional time reduction: ~4 years
- Additional interest savings: ~$110,000

Step 3: Annual Lump Sum Payments

Homeowner uses:

- $6,000 annual tax refund/bonus toward principal

Result:

- Additional time reduction: ~3 years
- Additional interest savings: ~$85,000

Step 4: Side Income Stream

Homeowner generates:

- $800 per month side income
- 100% directed to mortgage principal

Result:

- Additional time reduction: ~7 years
- Additional interest savings: ~$165,000

Step 5: Combined System Outcome

Total Impact:

- Original mortgage term: 30 years
- New mortgage payoff time: ~10 years and 8 months

Total Time Saved:

- Approximately 19 years

Total Interest Saved:

- Approximately $455,000

Key Insight

The power of this example is not any single strategy. It is the combination of all strategies working together:

- Payment timing (biweekly)
- Monthly extra cash flow
- Annual lump sums
- Side income
- Consistency over time

Each strategy alone produces meaningful results. But together, they completely transform the mortgage timeline.

Final Lesson

Mortgage freedom is not the result of one decision.

It is the result of a system.

When homeowners combine multiple strategies consistently over time, the mortgage stops being a 30-year burden and becomes a structured, manageable path to financial independence.

The system is what creates freedom.

Final Tips and Suggestions for Mortgage Freedom

How to Successfully Reach a Paid-Off Home Without Losing Your Lifestyle

Reaching mortgage freedom is not just a financial milestone—it is a structural shift in your entire life. When the mortgage disappears, so does one of the largest fixed obligations most households carry. That change impacts cash flow, stress levels, flexibility, retirement timing, investment capacity, and even decision-making freedom. However, the journey to mortgage freedom is where the real transformation happens, not just the final payoff moment.

The most important thing to understand is that mortgage freedom is not achieved through one dramatic action. It is achieved through hundreds of small, intentional decisions made consistently over time. Many homeowners underestimate this and look for shortcuts or extreme strategies that are difficult to maintain. In reality, the most successful mortgage payoff journeys are built on sustainability, discipline, and patience rather than intensity alone.

One of the strongest final recommendations is to focus on consistency over perfection. Many people start strong with extra payments, budgeting changes, or income strategies, but they stop when life becomes busy or unexpected expenses arise. This is normal. Financial systems are not meant to be perfect every month. They are meant to be resilient over years. A homeowner who makes moderate but consistent progress over ten to fifteen years will almost always outperform someone who starts aggressively but stops repeatedly.

Another critical tip is to avoid financial burnout. Mortgage payoff should never feel like punishment. If a strategy forces extreme lifestyle restriction, eliminates all enjoyment, or creates constant stress, it is unlikely to last. Sustainable financial success includes room for enjoyment, family experiences, travel, and mental peace. The goal is not to build a life you want to escape from while paying off your mortgage. The goal is to build a life you enjoy while strategically reducing debt.

A powerful mindset shift is to stop thinking in terms of restriction and start thinking in terms of direction. Instead of asking "What do I have to give up?" ask "Where should my money go to create the best long-term outcome?" This subtle change transforms mortgage payoff from a sacrifice into a strategy. You are not losing money—you are redirecting it toward ownership and freedom. Another essential tip is to always maintain emergency savings while accelerating mortgage payoff. One of the most common mistakes homeowners make is putting every available dollar toward their mortgage while ignoring liquidity. Life is unpredictable. Medical bills, car repairs, job changes, and family emergencies happen. Without reserves, homeowners often end up relying on credit cards or loans, which can reverse progress quickly. A balanced approach protects both your progress and your stability.

It is also important to recognize that mortgage freedom is not an all-or-nothing goal. Many homeowners believe they must either aggressively pay off their mortgage or ignore it completely. In reality, there are many levels in between. Even small extra payments consistently applied can make a meaningful difference over time. A few hundred dollars per month may not feel significant, but over years it can remove substantial time and interest from a loan.

Another key suggestion is to automate as much as possible. Human behavior is inconsistent, but systems are reliable. Automation removes emotional decision-making and ensures progress continues even when motivation is low. Setting up automatic extra principal payments, scheduled transfers to savings, or direct allocation of side income can dramatically improve long-term consistency. The less you rely on willpower, the more likely you are to succeed. Homeowners should also avoid comparing their journey to others. Financial timelines vary based on income, expenses, family size, interest rates, and personal goals. Some people can aggressively pay off mortgages in a short period. Others need a slower, more balanced approach. Comparison often leads to frustration or unrealistic expectations. The only meaningful comparison is your current financial position versus your past position.

Another important tip is to use windfalls strategically. Tax refunds, bonuses, commissions, and unexpected income should not be automatically absorbed into lifestyle spending. Even allocating a portion of windfalls toward principal reduction can create massive long-term benefits. These irregular payments often produce disproportionate impact because they reduce principal immediately without affecting monthly living standards.

It is also wise to periodically reassess your mortgage strategy. Life changes over time. Income increases, expenses shift, interest rates change, and personal goals evolve. A strategy that made sense five years ago may not be optimal today. Reviewing your plan once or twice per year helps ensure that your mortgage payoff strategy remains aligned with your current situation. One of the most overlooked tips is to focus on increasing income instead of only cutting expenses. Expense reduction has limits, but income potential is often expandable. Even modest side income streams, overtime work, freelance projects, consulting, or monetizing skills can significantly accelerate mortgage payoff when applied intentionally. The goal is not to work endlessly, but to strategically increase cash flow where possible.

Another important concept is psychological reinforcement. Mortgage payoff is a long journey, and motivation will naturally fluctuate. Tracking progress visually can make a significant difference. Seeing the balance decrease faster, watching interest savings accumulate, or marking milestones creates emotional reinforcement that supports continued discipline.

It is also helpful to define what mortgage freedom actually means for you personally. For some, it means eliminating debt as quickly as possible. For others, it means reducing it significantly while still investing and maintaining flexibility. There is no single correct definition. Clarity of purpose makes execution easier because you are not constantly second-guessing your decisions.

Homeowners should also be careful not to over-optimize every financial decision. Some people become so focused on efficiency that they lose enjoyment of life. Financial freedom is not about squeezing every possible dollar into debt reduction.

It is about creating a better life both now and in the future. A balanced approach ensures that progress does not come at the cost of happiness.

Another key recommendation is to treat mortgage payoff as part of a larger wealth strategy. Eliminating a mortgage is powerful, but it should not come at the expense of retirement planning, emergency savings, or investment opportunities. True financial strength comes from balance across multiple areas, not perfection in one.

As homeowners get closer to paying off their mortgage, it is important to plan ahead for what comes next. Many people experience a temporary loss of direction after becoming debt-free. Without a mortgage payment, there is suddenly additional cash flow available each month. Planning how to use that money in advance helps prevent lifestyle inflation and ensures continued wealth-building momentum.

A common recommendation is to immediately redirect former mortgage payments toward investing, savings, or other wealth-building goals. This creates a powerful compounding effect where the discipline built during mortgage payoff continues to benefit long after the mortgage is gone.

Another final suggestion is to maintain humility throughout the process. Financial success is not permanent unless it is managed well. Markets change, life circumstances evolve, and unexpected events occur. Staying disciplined, avoiding overconfidence, and continuing to make thoughtful decisions ensures that mortgage freedom leads to lasting financial security rather than temporary relief.

Ultimately, mortgage freedom is not just about eliminating debt. It is about building a system of financial behavior that creates long-term stability, flexibility, and opportunity. The strategies in this series are not designed for quick fixes. They are designed for transformation over time.

When applied consistently, even simple strategies can create extraordinary outcomes. Small extra payments, thoughtful refinancing, intentional income growth, disciplined cash flow management, and balanced investing all work together to reshape financial futures.

The most important takeaway is this: you do not need perfect timing, perfect income, or perfect conditions to achieve mortgage freedom. You only need consistent action, clear priorities, and a long-term mindset.

Financial freedom is built gradually, not suddenly. And every step you take in the right direction compounds into a stronger future.

What Happens When You Combine Everything Over Time

Let's look at a realistic full-life scenario showing how consistent application of multiple strategies leads to mortgage freedom.

Original Mortgage Scenario

- Loan Amount: $420,000
- Interest Rate: 6.25% fixed
- Loan Term: 30 years
- Monthly Payment: Approximately $2,590
- Total Interest Over Life of Loan: Approximately $514,000

Now let's apply a realistic combination of strategies over time.

Strategy 1: Consistent Extra Monthly Payment

- Extra $300 per month toward principal

Result:

- Mortgage reduced by ~4.5 years
- Interest saved: ~$95,000

Strategy 2: Biweekly Payment Structure

- Equivalent of 13 payments per year

Result:

- Additional ~4 years reduced
- Interest saved: ~$80,000

Strategy 3: Annual Lump Sum (Tax Refund/Bonus)

- $5,000 per year applied to principal

Result:

- Additional ~3 years reduced
- Interest saved: ~$75,000

Strategy 4: Side Income ($600/month average)

- Fully applied to mortgage

Result:

- Additional ~7 years reduced
- Interest saved: ~$145,000

Combined Outcome

Total Results:

- Original Loan Term: 30 years
- New Loan Term: ~11 years and 6 months

Total Time Saved:

- Approximately 18.5 years

Total Interest Saved:

- Approximately $395,000

Final Insight

This example demonstrates a powerful truth:

No single strategy creates mortgage freedom alone.

It is the combination of:

- Consistency (monthly payments)
- Structure (biweekly system)
- Discipline (lump sums)
- Growth (side income)

Working together over time that creates transformational results.

Final Lesson of the Series

Mortgage freedom is not about doing one big thing. It is about doing many small things correctly for a long time. When you combine discipline, strategy, and consistency, the mortgage stops being a lifelong burden...and becomes a temporary chapter in your financial story.

www.ingramcontent.com/pod-product-compliance
Lightning Source LLC
LaVergne TN
LVHW040519210926
848480LV00007BA/1512
9798256007317